W9-BLV-194

Practicing
Rural Social Work

Advisory Editor
Thomas M. Meenaghan, *New York University*

Related books of interest

RURAL SOCIAL WORK IN THE 21ST CENTURY
Michael R. Daley

ESSENTIAL SKILLS OF SOCIAL WORK PRACTICE:
Assessment, Intervention, and Evaluation, Second Edition
Thomas O'Hare

THE PRACTICE OF SOCIAL WORK IN NORTH AMERICA:
Culture, Context, and Competency Development
Kip Coggins

NAVIGATING HUMAN SERVICE ORGANIZATIONS, Third Edition
Rich Furman and Margaret Gibelman

WRITING CLEARLY FOR CLIENTS AND COLLEAGUES:
The Human Service Practitioner's Guide
Natalie Ames and Katy FitzGerald

THE COMMUNITY NEEDS ASSESSMENT WORKBOOK
Rodney A. Wambeam

SURVIVING DISASTER:
The Role of Social Networks
Robin L. Ersing and Kathleen A. Kost

ADVOCACY PRACTICE FOR SOCIAL JUSTICE, Third Edition
Richard Hoefer

MODERN SOCIAL WORK THEORY, Fourth Edition
Malcolm Payne

Practicing
Rural Social Work

Paul Force-Emery Mackie
Minnesota State University, Mankato

Kimberly Zammitt
Minnesota State University, Mankato

Michelle Alvarez
Southern New Hampshire University

LYCEUM
BOOKS, INC.

5758 South Blackstone Avenue
Chicago, Illinois 60637

© 2016 by Lyceum Books, Inc.

Published by
LYCEUM BOOKS, INC.
5758 S. Blackstone Avenue
Chicago, Illinois 60637
773-643-1903 fax
773-643-1902 phone
lyceum@lyceumbooks.com
www.lyceumbooks.com

All rights reserved under International and Pan-American Copyright Conventions. No part of this publication may be reproduced, stored in a retrieval system, copied, or transmitted, in any form or by any means without written permission from the publisher.

6   5   4   3   2   16   17   18   19   20

ISBN 978-1-933478-71-5

Printed in the United States of America.

Library of Congress Cataloging-in-Publication Data

Mackie, Paul Force-Emery, 1968-
 Practicing rural social work / Paul Force-Emery Mackie, Minnesota State University, Mankato, Kimberly Zammitt, Minnesota State University, Mankato, Michelle Alvarez, Southern New Hampshire University.
 pages cm
 Includes bibliographical references.
 ISBN 978-1-933478-71-5 (pbk. : alk. paper)
 1. Social service, Rural. I. Zammitt, Kimberly. II. Alvarez, Michelle. III. Title.
HV67.M33 2016
361.3'2091734--dc23
2015030947

Contents

Preface

The challenges and complexities associated with practicing social work in rural areas have long been discussed, debated, addressed, and pondered. In fact, a considerable amount of social work and behavioral health literature has been generated addressing this topic and surely this will continue to be an area of dialogue, perhaps in perpetuity—but why? Why is rural social work practice sometimes seen as so complex and difficult to understand outside of the generally recognized challenges associated with any helping profession? Historically, one needs not look far to find evidence of discussions in the literature, ranging from asking the seemingly simple question of what "rural" is and isn't, to asking if rural social work practice differs in a meaningful way from practicing with more urban-based clientele. While these and other related debates continue, the overall theme remains constant: A legitimate argument can be made that practicing social work in rural areas is different enough to justify our efforts to focus on developing deeper and more sophisticated understandings around it.

Practicing Rural Social Work was written from a systems-theory, strengths-based approach to serve as a source of information for students, practitioners, and educators seeking to further develop social work knowledge, skills, and abilities as they apply to practicing in rural areas; this text is oriented toward helping rural social workers practice better. That said, it is not, nor could any single text be, a complete and all-inclusive source of information for rural social workers. Not unlike the broad and open rural landscapes we are describing in a geographic sense, rural social workers typically work in locations that include large spaces and sparse populations, and the topic is simply too broad and complex to capture all possible scenarios, situations, potential ethical dilemmas, and service needs. However, from a generalist model of practice approach and through the application of systems and person-in-environment theories, the authors expect that readers will develop a more sophisticated understanding of general problems and concerns commonly found in rural practice, and thus be better prepared to address these needs. The uniqueness of rural social work practice from micro, mezzo, and macro systems is addressed. From a practice perspective, we often ask how these systems interface and support each other from a systems approach but then fail to investigate the details of these interlocking and related systems more purposefully. Within this context, the uniqueness of rural practice with individuals, small groups, and communities is discussed, with examples provided to assist in developing a stronger understanding about the complexities of practice within each and among all.

We acknowledge that practicing social work in rural and otherwise isolated geographic regions differs from practicing in more populated areas. By why is it different? What makes "rural practice" so different from "urban practice"? Is it the lack of resources in one place versus having access to services in another? Is it the sociocultural and economic differences between and within groups, subcultures, and populations? Is it how we deliver services or which practice approaches we choose to accept or reject? Could identifying and addressing rural challenges be as simple as addressing transportation problems, improving economic conditions, and increasing access to social services and behavioral health services? These are common questions we attempt to answer in ways that encourage critical thinking, careful reflection, and self-directed learning so as to encourage real, positive, sustainable social change in rural environments.

It is the hope and expectation of the authors that upon completing this text, readers will be better grounded in their understanding of the complexities of rural social work practice and, as a result, be better prepared for the challenges that lie ahead for those who will eventually join the ranks of rural social workers. From the systems and ecological theoretical positions and person-in-environment and strengths perspectives, we argue that to truly respond to the well-being of rural residents, we need to learn to identify and implement opportunities for growth, development, health, and welfare. Here is where we will find room for real change in rural places. Given the uniqueness of rural places and the people who live in them, perhaps the more important hope among the authors is to encourage rural social workers to consider new and dynamic ways to deliver services effectively. The strength of rural areas is ultimately found in people's ability to adapt and conform to ever-changing environments, be they social, political, or physical. Rural social workers are most effective and successful when they recognize that those who live in rural places experience life differently from those in more populated places and that this reality is ultimately a strength and not a deficit.

This book was developed in response to a need for a more practice-oriented text to be used in the classroom where future rural social workers are being prepared, as well as in the field among those already engaged in this work. To complete this project, many individuals were integral in the process. The authors would like to thank all of those who carefully and thoughtfully reviewed the manuscript and offered insights, suggestions, and critiques that made the book a stronger and more relevant document. The authors would also like to thank editor and publisher David Follmer for his kind words of encouragement, support, and belief in this book, as well as his staff who edited this document and provided insights to improve it. We would like to extend our appreciation to all of our social work and behavioral health colleagues who over the years have kept the rural conversation alive and relevant, especially among those affiliated with the National Association for Rural Mental Health and the Rural Social Work Caucus. The contributions to rural scholarship and dialogue of members of these organizations cannot be overstated. A special and enduring thank-you is extended to Dr. Leon Ginsberg. Without Dr. Ginsberg's tireless focus on rural social issues, his many scholarly contributions, and his commitment to advancing rural social work knowledge over the years, books such as this may not have been possible. Special admiration goes out to the social workers who contributed case study examples found throughout this book. The stories and information they share enhance the information provided and offer readers "real world" insights into their experiences. Finally, the authors wish to acknowledge and sincerely thank all of the social workers and behavioral health professionals who practice every day in rural and frontier areas to improve the lives of others. Without them, there would be little point in our efforts as writers, researchers, and educators. We are sincerely grateful for their dedication and commitment to rural America.

1

Introduction to Rural Social Work

Practicing rural social work is unique in that rural areas are often difficult to define and cultural processes and life ways differ from what is commonly found in more urbanized locations. Further, the population of rural America currently accounts for less than 20 percent of the overall population of the United States, and this number continues to fall over time (Rural Assistance Center, 2015). In short, rural residents typically live life differently than do urban residents, and a smaller overall percentage of the United States population are living with these shared experiences. At the moment one begins to recognize the barriers associated not only with providing care generally, but with the added challenges associated with geographic distance, isolation, culture, ethnicity, social styles, and commonly held political ideologies, we begin to see that practicing social work in rural places is different. But what are these differences? How do they look, how do they manifest in the day-to-day lives of frontline workers and supervisors? According to York, Denton, and Moran (1989), the answer is that there is, in fact, little overall difference in professional characteristics or treatment modalities applied. They argued that, by and large, a social worker in a rural area will largely practice with the same general set of skills as someone working in an urban location. These authors argue that treatment modalities are essentially the same regardless of where they are geographically applied. However, others such as Hargrove (1982) and Mermelstein and Sundet (1977) argued in the contrary. Here, rural social work is viewed as different enough from urban practice to justify continued investigation of the phenomena. Those who feel that rural practice is in fact different approach the same question from a different perspective. The position is less focused on the question of whether or not similar practice modalities are applied (they essentially are) and more on how different practice approaches are applied.

To be fair, both positions are essentially correct, just from different perspectives. York, Denton, and Moran (1989) assert that when a rural social worker goes out to practice, they apply the same skills as those of their urban counterparts. The generalist approach to providing services is broad and, as such, includes the application of a wide variety of approaches, concepts, and skills. For example, when a social worker determines the best therapeutic intervention treatment plan for a particular consumer includes cognitive behavioral therapy, this would be an appropriate treatment approach regardless of where the consumer resides. However, supporters of the notion that rural practice is notably different are also correct. Geographic isolation, driving time, problems and challenges associated with dual relationships, cultural concerns, and localized sociopolitical perceptions all complicate the delivery and distribution of services. Complications common in any social work practice regardless of location are all too often amplified on the rural landscape. Imagine you determine that a consumer may be best served using cognitive behavioral therapy. You and your client map out a plan to meet once a week for the next ten weeks to address the condition. In a rural area this requires them to come to your office, which is well known in the local community. People know the social services office, and they also know each other, what they drive, where they live, and who they associate with in the community. This doesn't imply that everyone knows everything about each other, but that enough people know enough about others that it's difficult or even impossible to "hide" much information from the larger community. Consumers express concern that they or even their cars will be recognized parked at the social services office and fear that stigmatization may occur. In short, they are reluctant to receive services due to the concern that in places where confidentiality is difficult to maintain, their identity may be breached. In response, your alternative suggestion is to meet them at their residence, but the concern remains in play because you will drive your marked county social services car and park it in their driveway and people may see it from the road. Given these valid concerns, now the question is, How does one go about providing services in rural areas in such a way that recognizes the unique characteristics and needs of consumers and at the same time provides the needed care? There is no definitive answer to this conundrum, but opportunities exist to meet consumers' needs while, at the same time, maintain their confidentiality. For example, you may be able to meet with them in a third-party location (for example, at a physicians' clinic or a school), drive an unmarked car, or even refer them to a provider in a different community. While these may or may not be viable options given unique situations, what is most important is to be able to recognize that confidentiality and identities in rural areas are often issues that require unique attention, and one needs to be creative in how these concerns are addressed. Awareness of this is critical to providing appropriate and ethical care in this environment.

Rural social workers often have fewer resources to draw upon, creating a need to maintain a broad range of skills and abilities. In addition, these same rural workers are likely to address a wide variety of social concerns and are less likely to have professional contacts and support compared to urban workers (Daley, 2015; Jerrell, 1983). Imagine the life of a rural child welfare or school worker. In this capacity, one is privileged to considerable information about people in the community and will need to keep that information in confidence. In more populated areas, this social worker would likely have a fair amount of access to an array of services consumers need, such as housing assistance, transportation, food stability, financial aid, addiction services, nutrition needs, tutoring, and access to psychiatrists, psychologists, and health care professionals. Depending on the remoteness of their location, rural social workers may have only limited access to services and, at times, no services immediately available. Therefore, the need to be creative is further compounded, within the scope and parameters of the practitioner's skills and abilities. At this point the rural social worker needs to draw upon his or her critical thinking skills, creativity, and ability to prioritize what is most important to address and seek innovative ways to meet consumer needs. To illustrate, too often there is a lack of crisis behavioral health services available in rural communities. However, most areas do have access to hospitals or clinics. A creative and innovative approach to addressing problems associated with a lack of crisis services is to work with members of the health care delivery system and develop a response system or process that addresses the most critical elements, then develop how to best follow up with these services through the same or other providers. What is most important is keeping the best interests of consumers at the forefront of the conversation and being innovative in best meeting their needs.

DEFINING RURAL

One of the first questions that emerges when one begins to discuss rural social work practice is, what is rural? How do we define it? Does "rural" remain constant over time, or do definitions change? Understanding this question is important in that how we conceptualize the term guides who we serve, how we address policy, and even how we practice. Beyond this general definition, operationally defining what is (and is not) "rural" has evolved into a complicated discussion. However, there are several definitions available, and each has distinct benefits and limitations.

The United States Census Bureau (2015a) defines "rural" by regional population density, the region's proximity to urban centers, and the overall population size of a particular region. For example, the Census Bureau considers an urbanized area as one that has fifty thousand or more total people residing in both the "large city" and thesurrounding regions. This definition considers the "urban" area broadly; it is the sum total of population of the general region. In addition, this definition includes consideration of a population density that has one thousand or more persons per square mile (Ciarlo & Zelarney, 2000). In contrast, the Federal Office of Management and Budget (OMB) breaks down the differences based on two distinct terms: a nonmetropolitan statistical area (non-MSA) and a metropolitan statistical area (MSA). Here, the OMB defines non-MSAs and MSAs by county population and considers a county as nonrural when the county contains a city of fifty thousand or more in population, and a total broader population of one hundred thousand or more. To complicate the measurement further, the OMB takes into consideration the distance of commuting to work as a factor as well (Ciarlo & Zelarney, 2000).

Another two approaches used to measure "rural" are each sponsored by the United States Department of Agriculture (USDA). The first is the Economic Research Service's (ERS) Rural–Urban Continuum Code; the second is the Urban Influence Code. Both of these definitions expand beyond the dichotomy of a location being either rural or urban, which is largely how the OMB defines the differences. For example, the USDA ERS Rural–Urban classification focuses on rural and urban definitions by breaking them down on a continuum from the largest metropolitan areas (for example, Chicago or New York City) to communities smaller than twenty-five hundred persons that are also not adjacent to a metropolitan area. In contrast, the USDA Urban Influence Code defines the largest metropolitan areas as counties with a population of over one million, ranging down to counties that do not have a city of at least twenty-five hundred people and are not adjacent to a metropolitan area (see Ciarlo & Zelarney, 2000). In addition, the USDA ERS has also developed a third classification of measuring "rural" based largely on socioeconomic characteristics. Here, eleven different types of nonmetropolitan counties are further defined from economic and policy perspectives. This allows the definition to recognize the diversity of social and economic structures across rural space (Cook & Mizer, 1994). There are benefits and challenges to each of the ways of defining what is and isn't rural. For the purposes of many, simply creating a dichotomous "urban" versus "nonurban" (meaning a location is defined as rural by default) designation is satisfactory. However, when attempting to better understand the demographics of regions that contain some but not all levels of services, applying a more nuanced, continuum-oriented approach may be more appropriate.

What is most important is finding designations that best represent what resources are available in such a way as to identify areas of need toward which to best direct services.

Given all of the choices of definition stated here, it is understandable that many find the process of defining rural at best complex and at worst frustrating. To complicate the discussion further is the concept of "frontier" rural status within the general, overarching concept of rural. "Frontier" rural is a special designation that is defined by extremely low population density, consisting of fewer than seven persons per square mile (Ricketts, 1999). Understandably, this represents the "most rural" areas of rural America. Problems associated with providing all types of human services become amplified here. For example, frontier status counties primarily exist in the western United States, beginning with the prairie states and extending to near the Pacific coastline. These are geographically isolated regions that are represented by the "big open country" of the Great Plains across the Rocky Mountains to the western slope of the continental divide. To say that nobody lives in this geographic landscape is obviously inaccurate; of course people live in frontier America. Like all people, those who live in these areas at times are also in need of social services and health care no differently from those living in more populated regions.

While different definitions are available for conducting more distinct and nuanced local analysis of rural space and populations, the generally accepted rural population in the United States is slightly less than 20 percent of the total overall population today (Rural Assistance Center, 2015). However, it is important to note that Ginsberg (2011) conducted a review of the literature and suggests that the population of rural America lies somewhere between 20 and 25 percent or 60–75 million people. Additionally, Daley (2015) explains that the number of rural residents is growing in actual numbers; however because the population is increasing faster in urban areas than it is in rural ones, the overall percentage difference between rural and urban residents is smaller and continues to fall. Even so, rural geographical areas account for approximately 80 percent of total landmass. These numbers show that regardless of the definition applied, rural residents account for a considerable minority of the total population, though, at the same time, they stretch across the majority of the United States landmass. In short, there are simply fewer people spread out across a broader landscape. This isolation can be viewed from two different perspectives. First, there are the problems associated with geographic distance such as transportation difficulties and acquiring goods and services due to distances between resources. Second, challenges associated with social, political, economic, and cultural isolation must always be considered. Often, both of these considerations combine to create even more complex situations. For example, Oglala Lakota (formerly Shannon) County, South Dakota, is one of the poorest counties in the United States (Lengerich, 2012) and is located entirely within the Pine Ridge Indian Reservation. Based on 2013 data, this county has about fourteen thousand residents, of which 93 percent identify as American Indian. The per capita annual income is approximately $8,768 per year, and over 53 percent of county residents live below the poverty line (US Census, 2015b). With a population distribution of only six persons per square mile, Oglala Lakota County, South Dakota, is considered a "frontier" county (Ciarlo & Zelarney, 2000), meaning it is a largely unpopulated place with few people living across a broad landscape that has the additional issues associated with diverse populations. This serves as a stark example of isolation on many different levels that, when combined, speaks loudly to a constellation of issues that eventually leads to the reality of a rural place and people isolated from the realities of the broader society.

Another honest discussion to be held regarding the definition of *rural* surrounds the concept of perception. Mackie (2011) attempted to address this question by identifying that different regions of the United States and the people who reside in them perceive rural differently. For example, the western panhandle region of Nebraska is, by nearly all definitions, rural. However, a few communities such as Scottsbluff and Gering (with a combined population of about twenty-four thousand) exist as regional economic and activity centers. Relative to the area around it, they are largely perceived as at least urban-like, but perhaps only to those who reside in the larger geographic area. An Atlanta or Los Angeles resident might find it very difficult to consider the city of Scottsbluff as containing qualities and attributes of what would be found in more urban locations whereas someone from Bridgeport, Nebraska (population fifteen hundred and thirty-five miles away) might consider it much more urbanized. To put it simply, those living outside of Scottsbluff may consider it a "big town" with social and economic resources otherwise unobtainable elsewhere in the region regardless of whether it's a designated "urban" area or not. The important point of this discussion is to openly recognize and appreciate that while "rural" has specific and measurable definitions, there are simultaneously much more subjective definitions that impact decisions, attitudes, and perceptions regardless of the regional federal or state definition. This question of perception is very real, but too often overlooked. A rural social worker must develop a clear and sophisticated understanding of how a community views itself so as to better understand the geopolitical culture and attributes of the community or region.

EARLY HISTORY OF RURAL SOCIAL WORK

Understanding rural social work practice from a historical perspective is important so as to learn where we have been, where we are now, and where social work may be going in the future. There is no specific date when rural social work was specifically identified as a subarea under the umbrella of general social work. However, we may extrapolate from the available literature that rural social work language began to emerge early in the history of social work itself. For example, Jane Addams, considered the "mother" and founder of modern social work in the United States established the Settlement House movement in Chicago in 1889 (Popple & Leighninger, 2008). From here, the growth of social work as a profession grew into the dawn of the twentieth century. While it is recognized that social work as a discipline and profession grew from urban roots, it didn't take long for the term rural social work to begin to emerge in the literature, and by the 1920s through the 1940s it had grown into a distinct body of work. For example, Steiner (1921) discussed the need for rural-specific social work education to better prepare those who would eventually be employed in rural areas. At around the same time, Sanderson (1923) developed a discussion around the need for community organization as a rural social work activity. The author argues that for rural communities to be truly progressive, healthy, and meeting the needs of societal members, there needs to be a collective unified approach from within the community. Continuing on, Landis (1936) addressed rural socioeconomic conditions as they related to New Deal legislation and the era of the Great Depression. Landis outlined the social changes indicative of the times; shifting the expectation of assistance to the poor from community members as a private act to assistance being rendered from state and federal sources as a public act.

An important review of early professional social work and mental health care in rural areas was conducted by Swanson (1972). Swanson investigated rural social work from a historical perspective and focused on the development of the discipline in this area. The author describes how professional social work in the rural United States began in the nineteenth century as a response to social and economic concerns primarily in agricultural communities. Social workers initially focused on improvements in farm management, rural health, social welfare, improved education, and leadership skills (Swanson, 1972). One social leader of the time declared that the same social work problems existing in urban areas were also apparent in rural areas, but rural needs were overlooked because of the overly urban focus of social work (Bailey, 1908, as cited in Swanson, 1972). This is where, according to Swanson, one can find the apex of the debate between "social work in rural areas" versus "rural social work."

Swanson (1972) argued that in a historical sense professional social work had vacillated between being simply social work in rural areas and a defined professional form of "rural social work practice." Social work in rural areas was defined as the application of the discipline's philosophy and by interventions utilizing techniques grounded in urban social work practices. Conversely, rural social work became known as a subdiscipline within the field that has unique qualities with a specific focus on rural problems. For example, a movement for rural-specific social work grew out of the Red Cross Home Service during and after World War I to meet the needs of those suffering from the loss of primary wage earners to the war effort (Deacon, 1919, as cited in Swanson, 1972). During this time period, some rural states attempted to develop rural social work programs with varying degrees of success. For example, North Carolina, Iowa, and Minnesota all attempted to integrate social work in rural areas by placing social workers in rural places to address a variety of socioeconomic needs of residents.

North Carolina was attentive to the needs of this movement by requiring every county in the state to establish a welfare board and hire a social worker. These rural social workers were responsible for educational standards, probation, parole, family welfare programs, and child welfare (Swanson, 1972). By 1930, the concept of rural social work was well established. Professional schools of social work published articles and books aimed at preparing students specifically for rural practice (Swanson, 1972). By the early 1940s, the concept of rural social work was waning. It was soon to be replaced by urban concepts of treatment and intervention and the phrase "rural social work" was changed to "social work in rural areas." Swanson (1972) concludes that "rural social work disappeared because the social work profession quit identifying significant distinctions in rural work" (p. 526). Consequently, the belief in a fundamental rural–urban dichotomy all but disappeared from the field of social work.

Historically, others grappled with questions about rural social work and debated the meaning of it as well. For example, Matthews (1927) observed and discussed general differences between rural and urban social workers and how each practices. The author states that where the urban worker typically has a considerable bank of resources to draw upon, their rural counterpart rarely has such a luxury. The rural worker is very much a generalist practitioner and needs to develop a deeper, more complex understanding of the services available and how to tap into them in constructive and useful ways. Matthews refers to the rural worker as "the lone worker" stating that she will likely practice for days or even weeks at a time alone as, all too often, she is the only worker in her county or region.

Closely related, a rural social worker will also likely lack the continued professional support and guidance typically afforded to more urbanized colleagues. Professional supervision is rare, and training opportunities to remain updated on current best practices are at best, limited. Matthews advises the rural social worker to develop and maintain an understanding of the social, political, and economic structures and forces unique to rural and small communities. He also recommends that the rural worker develop skills that assist in facilitating volunteerism in the community, as these "informal" relationships are often the only real and tangible resources one may be able to tap into in remote geographic locations.

In 1926, Steiner discussed the complexities of rural social work practice. Similar to the work of Matthews (1927), Steiner (1926) identified several sociocultural and socioeconomic differences between rural and urban areas and how these differences manifested in rural and small communities. Steiner recommended that the rural worker seek out opportunities to link to resources with others, sometimes with more urban agencies if geographic distance allowed it, or with other rural agencies when necessary, to best provide services to the rural population. However, Steiner cautioned that rural social work practice not be viewed as a distinctive set of new or different techniques from those applied in urban settings, but as "extensive modifications" of practice and procedure to meet the variety of rural conditions. Steiner expresses a need to truly understand the culture and life ways of rural communities in such a way that allows for real change and improvement of social conditions to occur. In short, the rural social worker needs to carefully study all aspects of their ommunity to learn what is unique and what the community members are willing and able to embrace.

Given the historical information presented thus far, some important observations can be made. Fast forwarding to the present, many of the concerns expressed by rural social work researchers in the past remain relevant today. Understanding the community in which one lives and works continues to be paramount to being a successful rural social worker in our current times. While there is less overall economic impact from agriculture today than in the past, some areas continue to be deeply informed and influenced culturally as well as economically by this industry, and a community's identity is deeply embedded in it. Over time, however, we have witnessed a great migration from farming, lumbering, and mining communities to factory and other labor-centered economic activities in rural areas. Today, those industrial-based economies are giving way to more technological advances and the effects of economic globalization, which has again redefined the landscape of rural places (this is discussed in greater detail in Chapter 5). That said, the notion that there is a "rural culture" remains intact in that the concept of "rural" is still largely rooted in images of open landscapes, farms, mountains, deserts, and fields. In short—rural is still seen as "something in the country" even if that isn't really an accurate representation of the experiences of many people living in rural places today (Daley, 2015). To be successful, the rural social worker needs to embrace and understand these points and work to learn the nuances of what rural is and is not as well as what rural means to those living within the context and framework of the geography. To illustrate, we know that at the turn of the twenty-first century, agriculture did not look the way it did at the turn of the twentieth century. Today, farms are much more technologically focused, they are larger, and there are fewer people actively engaged in the direct practice of farming. That said, agriculture is still a powerful economic force in rural areas, especially in the Midwest and among many southern states. A large immigrant population (both legally and illegally in the United States) currently works in meatpacking plants, on large dairy and poultry farms, and in the harvest of fruits and vegetables. Agriculture in America is now large in scale and focuses more than ever on efficiency. As a result, social workers in these areas are responding to a very different set of community needs: bilingual education, the need for language interpreters, differing economic issues, challenges associated with the melting of cultures, and immigration issues. As one can see, being a rural social worker today requires skill sets not typically considered important in the past. Perhaps the most interesting part of this discussion is that rural areas have a history of being in flux around issues such as these. Rural areas have a long history of being places where immigration is common and economics challenging. Here is where having a sound understanding of differing theoretical perspectives, married to different practice approaches, can assist, clarify, and move us forward. Based on what we have learned here, when discussing rural social work knowledge, theory, and practice, the past is, more often than not, prologue.

PERCEPTIONS AND MISCONCEPTIONS OF RURAL LIFE

The image of life in rural America has long struggled with being perceived as idealistic, which is to say, there is a misconception in the minds of many that "rural" is a place where life is simple, quiet, and less strife-laden than life in urbanized areas (Ginsberg, 2011; Judd, Jackson, Komiti, Murray, Hodgins, & Fraser, 2002; Vidich & Bensman, 1960). However, evidence against this notion is well documented in reference to the needs and problems of farm families (Durham & Miah, 1993; Hsieh, Cheng, Sharma, Sanders, & Thiessen, 1989; Martinez-Brawley & Blundall, 1989), the rural homeless and those struggling to maintain housing stability (Green, Johnson, Bremseth, & Tracy, 1995; Hilton & DeJong, 2010; Nooe & Cunningham, 1992), poverty and its unique rural socioeconomic conditions (Scales & Streeter, 2004), and those experiencing alcohol and substance abuse (Fortney, Rost, Zhang, & Warren, 1999; Rost, Owen, Smith, & Smith, 1998).

Judd et al. (2002) suggested that there are five main reasons for misconceptions about rural life. First, these authors recognize that in the past, those writing and conversing about rural places have unrealistically idealized and romanticized rural life while at the same time, "demonizing" urban living. Rural places have often been portrayed and generalized as safe, happy, quiet places occupied by gentle people who generally act and think differently from people in more crowded spaces. In contrast, cities have as equally as often been cast as dangerous and forbidding places where people are cramped, aggressive, and relatively unhappy. This said, Judd et al. (2002) also (and perhaps more accurately) suggest that traditional social norms and values typically found in rural areas such as conservatism, religiousness, individualism, and community familiarity are not always necessarily positive, and may even contribute to the additional need for social services and behavioral health treatment. These authors are recognizing that rural places contain both good and bad attributes rather than casting a false image that fails to accurately represent the truth. Second, the authors found that overall, rural residents' physical health is often poorer than what is found among urban dwellers. They argue that given the interrelatedness between physical and mental health, it is possible that one may find lower mental health functioning in rural areas as a result. Third, rural life has changed considerably over the past several decades, especially since the "farm crisis" of the 1980s. Traditional characteristics such as personal independence, deep-seated social norms based on religious beliefs, and local culture once commonly found in these regions are weaker than in the past due to the increased encroachment of suburbanization into what was once rural landscape. Fourth, the authors suggest that studies associated with rural social services in the past have been methodologically flawed, as many were based on convenience samples rather than large and more randomly sampled research, and what have been considered "best practices" in these areas may not actually be best or even appropriate. Finally, much of the past research focused primarily on quantity questions such as the prevalence of social service needs and psychological disorders among rural and urban locations. While having a sound understanding of the prevalence of particular occurrences, this information needs to advance in such a way that it focuses on developing strategies for better care and resource allocation. It is important to note that each of these observations focuses largely on negatives and even stereotypes often associated with living in rural areas. It is true that negatives abound and are of critical concern to all. However, there are also many positives—strengths within the rural literature that merit further exploration and discussion.

In contrast to the Judd et al. (2002) findings, Mackie and Simpson (2007) studied questions surrounding social work students and their desire to live and work in rural areas after college graduation. The authors found that students from rural areas viewed the rural lifestyle as more attractive and more appealing and expressed greater interest in living in a rural setting compared to students raised in more urban environments. Additionally, in a survey of social workers currently living in and practicing in rural areas, Mackie (2007) found that those who were originally from rural areas had completed a rural practicum as a social work student, and those who were purposefully exposed to rural-specific content as students were more likely to seek out rural social service employment opportunities than those who did not hold these characteristics. From these studies, it appears that familiarity is an important concept to consider. Individuals from rural areas and those who were, in a sense, acculturated to the life ways of rural living consider themselves more likely to eventually gravitate to rural locations. However, this information does not negate the value of Judd et al.'s (2002) suggestion that sociocultural life ways and belief systems often found in rural areas may limit individual, family, and community growth and development.

A seminal work on the topic of rural life comes from the sociological team of Arthur Vidich and Joseph Bensman. Vidich and Bensman (1960) conducted a three-year qualitative study that culminated in the book, *Small Town in Mass Society*. The authors lived in a rural community of approximately twenty-five hundred people in upstate New York, and studied the dynamics of rural life and culture. They found that "Springdale" (a fictitious name to protect the true identity of the community) residents were especially suspect of other communities when people from outside of the community exposed their town's shortcomings. When social concerns about potentially politically charged issues such as poor schools or criminal activity emerged, Springdale residents responded by saying they could deal with the problems more efficiently and effectively than outsiders. They even discounted the severity of their problems, arguing that the problems were external, the fault of outside influences, and not troubles that were born internally. Stigmatizing and negative perceptions about the community or individuals were taken seriously and avoided when possible. This type of denial in rural areas not only exacerbated original problems and reduced opportunities to honestly address needs in constructive ways, but also served as an example of how the seemingly unflappable idyllic life of rural

America is deeply imbedded in the psyche of rural and urban dwellers alike.

Between 1960 and 1968, CBS aired *The Andy Griffith Show* on American television. The sitcom revolved around the relatively quiet life and times of a small-town sheriff and his clumsy but well-meaning deputy. Set in the fictional community of Mayberry, North Carolina, viewers experienced a rural place where things were simple, honest, and charming. It was a place where, by and large, people got along, the town was essentially free of crime, the local barbershop was the center of gossip and politics, and, when someone in the community was having a hard time, community members naturally stepped in to help. There was little need for formalized social services or structured interventions because in places like Mayberry, kindly people looked out for each other. The result is what is colloquially referred to as the "Mayberry syndrome." The aptly named Mayberry syndrome is an important issue to consider in the provision and distribution of social services in rural communities. According to Lovelace (1995), the Mayberry syndrome is a phenomenon by which residents believe they know the business and activities of others due to the lack of social anonymity more often afforded to urban dwellers. Because the details of one's personal life are known by the community, the stigma associated with receiving formalized social services becomes compounded and, as a result, produces negative effects. For example, an individual might experience multiple and complex biopsychosocial challenges associated with an addiction. Seeking help for alcoholism in a small community could include attending Alcoholics Anonymous meetings in a local church basement or community center, but by attending these meetings, other community members will immediately know who the person is and the hope of "anonymity" is immediately gone. Using another illustration, imagine the differences between rural and urban places where simply parking one's car can raise curiosity or suspicion. In a small town where people often recognize one another by the vehicle they drive, parking the car in front of the social services office could indicate that services are being received, especially if that social services office is otherwise isolated in a particular part of a street or neighborhood. Moreover, a social worker can compromise anonymity simply by parking their (or an agency-marked) vehicle in a driveway. In rural areas, people are skilled at pulling information from multiple sources and (rightly or wrongly) drawing conclusions. In short, when most people know that Alcoholics Anonymous meetings are held each Thursday night in the basement of the local Lutheran church, that church does not hold services on Thursday nights, and your car is in that parking lot—you are at that meeting (whether you are or not).

To address this problem, Lovelace encourages rural social workers to develop community outreach programs, be aware of behavioral health issues and how they are addressed in medical settings (typically by primary care physicians), work with teachers to identify and help children in need of care, and develop self-help groups (thus building on the capital of informal helping systems), while, at the same time, recognize how the mechanics of public space operate and work to ensure confidentiality as best as they can. Applying these approaches may in turn encourage communities to establish some control over local mental health issues, community needs, and services, and, at the same time, potentially reduce the negative effects of social and culturally based stigma often associated with receiving services in rural communities.

Rural places are not as idyllic as often portrayed in cultural mediums like television, but that is not to say that shows like *The Andy Griffith Show* of the 1960s, *Hee Haw* of the 1970s, *The Dukes of Hazzard* of the 1980s, or *Northern Exposure* of the 1990s were complete lifestyle parodies. They did, in fact, capture certain attributes (both positive and negative) of rural life and expanded on those in such a way that they are now the images many have about living in the country. While rural encompasses both grand and subtle beauty where people often do know each other and are aware of community strengths and weaknesses across all systems levels, it is too often misrepresented through the media—which further feeds public misperceptions. It is important to always remember that less than 20 percent of Americans live in rural places. The majority of the US population likely does not consider rural areas in the same context as rural residents do. This becomes especially important in the areas of public policy, where too often rural communities lack voice, power, and influence. To be truly effective, the rural social worker must be able to identify these elements and maximize the strengths, while, at the same time, work within the structures that perpetuate the weaknesses. In short, rural social workers often face the reality that they are a voice for rural places and should work to address and correct misrepresentations, stereotypes, and inaccurate portrayals of rural life.

GUIDING THEORETICAL FRAMEWORKS

To fully understand and appreciate social work practice in the rural context, it is extremely important to understand basic theoretical approaches that apply to and guide practice. But what is a theory? According to *The Social Work Dictionary* (Barker, 2004), a theory is "a group of related hypotheses, concepts, and constructs, based on facts and observations that attempt to explain a particular phenomenon" (p. 434). While adequate, this is not the only definition available. Greene (2000) provides an excellent overview of several definitions; each offers a unique description that aids learners with arriving at a better understanding of the term. For example, Chess and Norlin (1988) describes theory as something that "offers an explanation for an idea and a set of related assumptions and concepts that explain a phenomenon being observed. Theory should give meaning and clarity to what otherwise would appear to be specific and isolated cases" (Greene, 2000, p. 5). Additionally, Shaw and Costanzo (1982) are credited with stating that "theories allow us to organize our observations and to deal meaningfully with information that would otherwise be chaotic and useless. Theory allows us to see relationships among facts and to uncover implications that otherwise would not be evident in isolated pieces of data" (Greene, 2000, p. 5). Given what we have learned here, theories are in essence ways of compiling ideas in such a way as to develop and advance further inquiry into human behavior and how people act within and across complex systems. The practice of rural social work is uniquely focused on working across and within complex systems in such a way as to identify needs, improve lives, and strengthen human services. To accomplish these goals, rural social workers must be well grounded in a wide variety of theoretical approaches.

To simplify this otherwise complicated area of theoretical scholarship and thought, two applicable theoretical positions are discussed here: ecological theory and systems theory. In addition, the persons-in-environment (PIE) perspective is discussed. While not a fully developed theory, it is a useful classification system used to identify and address social functioning problems. Each is commonly discussed within the social work literature, and each serves to guide our insights, direct our inquiry, and assist us in developing a deeper understanding around the complexities of social service practice. They allow us to include the magnitude of general questions about our social environment, but also to focus on more specific areas within, such as how we think and practice in rural areas.

SYSTEMS THEORY

Broadly defined, social work focuses on interactions and relationships between and among individuals, groups, organizations, and communities within their social, economic, political, and geographic environments. Systems theories, those that assist us in better understanding these relationships, are primarily grounded in three distinct systems levels: micro systems, mezzo systems, and macro systems. Understanding the interrelatedness of human actions and interactions within and across each of these systems is at the center of good social work practice. The application of generalist practice skills to pursue planned consumer changes in rural and small communities is even more critical from a systems perspective given the unique complexities of providing services across broad landscapes and, all too often, distant from a larger variety of service options. The application of systems theory provides the social worker a broad and dynamic approach to understanding a complex world.

The micro system primarily refers to the system that addresses the needs and concerns of individuals and immediate families. Here is where social workers are often seen practicing their craft. Providing one-on-one therapeutic services, developing treatment plans, working closely with families to address social needs, and serving as case workers are some of the most common duties of many social workers. That said, when viewed through a rural lens, providing macro level interventions immediately grows more complex. Imagine for a moment that you are working in a rural county as only one of a few (sometimes the only) social workers on staff. As a generalist practitioner, you face several different situations during the course of your workday. One client is in need of housing assistance, another has been referred to children's social services, and yet another is in need of substance abuse treatment. From a micro perspective, there may be a multitude of care options at your disposal. However, as a rural practitioner you also know that some are less available—and some may not be an option due to logistical difficulties. Therefore, you will need to be creative, skillful, and resourceful to meet the individual's needs. For example, Mackie (2012) found that in extremely rural areas of the Upper Peninsula of Michigan, social workers often find that they are unable to best serve youths in need of mental health services who are also deemed to be a danger to themselves or others. Because of the lack of services and resources, one could live as far as four hours from the nearest facility that specializes in such treatment. Imagine the multiple challenges associated with this situation. Can the family travel to this distant location, or do they lack transportation? If they do have transportation, can they afford the cost of fuel or to take the time off of work that will be associated with the travel? Once the otherwise seemingly simple issue of transportation is addressed (assuming that it was), you must consider other potential challenges such as questions regarding insurance payments, other costs associated with the treatment, and even the appropriateness of care. One must remember that in the attempt to get to treatment where options are limited, an assessment of the appropriateness of where the client is going is necessary. This has the potential to be a difficult decision at times as you work to balance the needs of the client with the availability of resources.

The mezzo system refers to the system of practice that focuses primarily with families, small groups (i.e., task groups), and organizations at the local level. Here, social workers often engage client systems to facilitate communication between and among groups, assist in mediation between stakeholders, and serve as negotiators addressing conflicting wants or needs. At the mezzo level, social workers are often charged with bringing people together in small groups with the purposeful goal of improving communications and interactions or relationships through mediation. To illustrate, rural social workers often find that, based on best practices, or due to limited resources, groups can be brought together to address social or community concerns. Consider how in a mezzo systems environment, divergent social groups may experience stress and pressure due to immigration into a rural community. Today, it's not uncommon to find communities struggling with a variety of ethnic migrations due to global political unrest (such as among Somali, Sudanese, and Hmong refugees) or as agricultural workers (such as Central and South American immigrants). The influx of people who might live differently and communicate with languages different than locally spoken can create friction. At the mezzo level, a rural social worker is uniquely qualified to address concerns through the development of community-based learning and listening sessions, a focus on the health and welfare of the new group through translators, and as advocates across a variety of situations.

The macro system refers to the system of practice that focuses on creating and sustaining positive change in the general society. Under this auspice, social workers engage in political action, administration, education, supervision, and community organizing. For example, social workers may engage in the political process through the application of policy development, analysis, and implementation. As an educator, social workers are found not only in the classroom teaching social work content, but also as supervising other social workers as subordinates and for licensure. Community organizing, one of the stalwart roles of the macro social worker, focuses on organizing neighborhood groups and communities, facilitating group work, and fostering networks in such a way as to advocate for and strengthen communities and members within them. Returning to the immigration example provided under the mezzo systems level discussion, one can see how a new population may experience a variety of challenges that go beyond the mezzo level. For example, broad housing needs, access to education, county or state policies, even federal laws may need to be redesigned, developed, or altered. In the most macro systems sense, international considerations may emerge. This could prove to be quite a task for a social worker and one should not expect to address these concerns alone. However, too often it's the social worker who is highly knowledgeable about the problems as well as skilled to formulate appropriate, multifaceted, and ethically grounded responses.

Combining each of these systems levels is paramount to the success of the social worker, especially among those who practice in rural areas. For example, a consumer in need of substance abuse services needs the care that micro practice provides. However, upon learning that there is a lack of support groups in the community (such as Alcoholics Anonymous or Narcotics Anonymous), the social worker may focus on developing this resource as well. Finally, one may find that, due to the lack of treatment facilities within a regionally appropriate space, there is a need to engage in the political process of advocating for funding to support the development and maintenance of such a facility. Given the isolation often associated with rural America, it is reasonable to conclude that there is a great need for these practitioners to be skilled as generalists and broad-systems focused social workers. Future chapters will address each system more specifically.

A Critique of Systems Theory

The theoretical ground of this text is based broadly on systems theory and how this approach to rural social work practice can be best understood. While many scholars across the vast plain of social sciences apply systems theory in intellectual areas such as this, others have made a fair and compelling case that this theory has limitations, especially when it is applied in rural places. Because these arguments are considered valid, and understanding possible weaknesses ultimately strengthens the ability to provide care, a critique of the theory is provided.

While there is some agreement that applying a systems theoretical model to understanding assists in maintaining homeostasis and balance (Green & Blundo, 1999), others argue that it can disrupt balance and actually create imbalance (Hudson, 2000). In fact, Leighninger (1977) argued that the critical challenge to general systems theory and how it is applied to social work practice is the problem of "assumed equilibrium." To Hudson, the idea that equilibrium actually exists is problematic, and while feedback loop changes in one system can and do impact other systems, there should be no assumption that even identified positive changes will result in other positive changes. In short, a positive change at one level may well have negative impacts in others.

Another challenge to systems theory focuses on the level of rationality expected by its users (Siporin, 1980). Even in environments where only a few social systems exist (such as is often found in rural regions), there is a multiplying effect that immediately complicates the ability to rationally understand and address the true nature of the problems identified (Hudson, 2000). This, coupled with the problem of assumed equilibrium creates the potential for an oversimplistic understanding of a problem, and changes that result can and will be superficial. For example, sometimes community members view clients or consumers of social services as needy, dependent, or any other negative identifier instead of equal members of society. When problems such as this are identified, do we ask "why are people in need of these services?" or "how might the community be contributing to these social problems?" This essentially leads to the question of blame—are people receiving services being blamed for their situation, is the community seeking to identify how structures within it may be contributing to the challenges, or both? From a systems theory perspective, questions such as these often remain as we look at the impact of one system on another without fully appreciating and understanding the complexities that exist between and within systems.

It is important to recognize limitations of theories, as all theories present with strengths and weaknesses. This short review of critiques of systems theory is not designed to dismantle the theory, but to express to the reader the importance of understanding how limitations at the theoretical level can create challenges at the practice level. For example, consider a macro level social work concern in a rural community in need of fire and emergency medical services. Community members recognize that these services are limited and want to increase the number of volunteer firefighting and emergency medical services (EMS) personnel. This, at one system level, is a good thing as it is likely that it will increase the quality of protection, security, and care of the community. However, moving forward with the "assumed equilibrium" that there are only positives and minimal or no negatives is a mistake. In this situation, the goal of increasing EMS or firefighting personnel may be simple in that people are available and willing to participate. However, there will be an increase in costs for additional equipment, training, insurance, and perhaps even infrastructure. To pay for these increases, the community may need to increase taxes or assess costs in other areas. If this cost is too high, people may experience problems associated with the loss of financial resources. If the cost for services becomes too high, community members may actually leave the area and, thus, reduce the original need to expand services. Beyond this, those most in need of the services the community is working to further develop may actually be those least able to pay for the increases in costs associated with the services (such as the very poor or elderly). It is important to understand that simply identifying areas where systems impact each other is not sufficient. The rural social worker must be able to expand his or her understanding and attempt to predict and forecast the impact of system changes across a variety of levels.

ECOLOGICAL THEORY

Ecological theory encourages us to consider social, environmental, and biological precepts that encourage our interest in the interconnections between social aspects of people (individually and collectively) and geographic factors. This theory focuses on factors that affect social functioning within a location context, meaning how people function based on ecological factors as well as personal causes of social problems (Hardcastle & Powers, 2004). For example, rural areas are influenced by terrain, social and physical isolation, and geographic location in ways dissimilar to what is found in more populated areas. Unlike more populated areas, an individual's access to care, dependence and interdependence on the land and weather, and economic factors fall within the parameters of consideration under this theoretical perspective. The ecological theoretical approach to understanding the practice of rural social work encourages us to consider the effects of geography, location, and the physical nature of the environment and the interconnectedness of each with those we seek to help. In short, we need to view rural social work practice as stemming from a place-as-location as much as from a people-in-location perspective.

PRACTICE MODELS FOR INTERVENTION

Practice models considered effective in understanding challenges associated with providing services in rural areas are the person-in-environment (PIE) and the strengths perspective. When viewing the unique challenges associated with living and working in rural areas, understanding of how people act and interact within their environment is paramount to understanding the relationship they have with each other. A sound understanding of the strengths perspective is also critical to the rural social worker, largely due to the need to be able to identify strengths of individuals, families, and communities. While it is true that people living in urban areas are dependent on each other, those living in rural areas are, and become more so, as populations are more isolated and dependent on the strengths, talents, and services of others.

Person-in-Environment

The person-in-environment practice model is a process for a classification system for social functioning problems; the PIE approach to understanding human connections and systems was initially developed as an alternative to the *Diagnostic and Statistical Manual of Mental Disorders* (DSM) (American Psychiatric Association, 2013). Understanding human actions through the use of the DSM is to do so by using the disease model. PIE is different in that it is at its foundation client centered rather than agency centered or disease-model based. This in turn supports two basic notions about social work as a practice: place the client at the center of the process and treatment, and apply an approach that supports communication and interaction across practice areas and expertise (Karis & Wandrei, 1996). This is not to suggest that the DSM is to be ignored or discounted, as this is an important and valued tool in social work practice. However, for the purposes of better understanding and responding to rural social service concerns, the PIE model is considered more inclusive of the multiple systems rural social workers regularly address in practice and practitioners should be as familiar with the PIE model as they often are with the DSM.

Like systems theory, the person-in-environment approach guides our understanding and interpretation of human behaviors and interactions in the social realm. Unlike systems theory, the PIE approach focuses on how people interact within and among the systems that encapsulate them. Where systems theory is more theoretical and generalist in nature, PIE is more specific and applicable to the people's individual needs and situations—the person-in-environment is both theoretical and prescriptive. From a theoretical perspective, this approach considers the dynamic relationships between individuals, families, groups, and communities and the environment in which they function. As a prescriptive approach, the person-in-environment approach provides a classification system where the practitioner can assess consumers' relationships using a codification approach and scoring matrix, which allows for defining specific areas where needs are specifically identified and addressed.

From the more theoretical perspective, Weiss-Gal (2008) defines PIE as "the person-in-environment approach views the individual and his or her multiple environments as a dynamic, interactive system, in which each component simultaneously affects and is affected by the other" (p. 65). It considers the person as a part of their environment, or system, which consists of the individual, each of the systems where the individual belongs, and the relationships and interrelationships contained within each system. As you can see, the person-in-environment approach is deeply embedded within the broader concepts of systems theory. However, it goes deeper in that all of the details of how one lives, interacts, and is reacted to within and among each system and the dynamic relationships between systems are explored. In short, applying the PIE perspective includes nearly all aspects of a person's life, as well as the environmental factors that influence his or her life.

From a more prescriptive view, PIE is built upon four discrete factors: Factor I identifies social role problems, Factor II addresses problems associated within the client's environment, Factor III focuses on a client's state of mental health, and Factor IV considers problems associated with an individual's mental health (Appleby, Colon, & Hamilton, 2007). While it is beyond the scope of this book to fully address this element of PIE, it is important to briefly describe the process.

According to Appleby, Colon, and Hamilton (2007), Factors I and II are most critical in the assessment of client systems, and we concur. Problems associated with an individual's social role in the broader society are critical to the understanding of their needs. For example, clearly identifying one's family, interpersonal relationships, occupations, and special life situation roles and the severity, duration, and coping processes associated can yield great insight that, in turn, leads to effective interventions. Germane to the topic of rural social work practice, Factor II (problems in the environment) includes nutrition, housing, economic resources, transportation, and discrimination, which are assessed for levels of severity and duration. Using the PIE assessment instrument, we can learn quickly and efficiently about the needs of individuals and their experiences within their environment. For example, economic resources and transportation problems are concerns that have been identified as important related to other issues often amplified in rural areas (poverty, spanning geographic distance). Also under Factor II, we can identify other areas of concern such as education, legal, health, safety, voluntary associations (sometimes referred to as "informal care systems"), and affectional support systems. All too often, rural social workers find themselves addressing these questions. For example, compared to urban dwellers, rural residents as a group have less education, have less access to health care and social services, and are more dependent on informal social support systems (i.e., churches, community-based services).

Strengths Perspective

Social work students are typically well versed in the *strengths perspective*, and, thus, practitioners in the field are commonly familiar with this concept. However, a review of this model is appropriate. The application of the strengths perspective for practicing in rural social work is both a philosophy and a practice model. This model builds on the view that clients contain within them resources that can assist them in improving their life conditions (Saleeby, 1997). Here, we do not begin from a position of client deficits but rather their strengths—we ask: What are they doing right and well as opposed to what are they doing wrong or poorly? From here, we can begin an investigation into strengths within them as individuals, families, groups, communities, and societies.

From a rural perspective, it can be very easy to fall into the trap of viewing social concerns through a deficits lens. If we begin from the position that people living in rural areas lack access to services and resources, we are doing so from a deficits position. We become focused on the lack of resources in schools, employment, hospitals, behavioral health and social services, and so on. However, from a strengths perspective we can look at the same problems and begin by seeking positive elements within the individual or community. For example, imagine you are working with an individual struggling with an alcohol addiction. You are more than aware that the nearest treatment facility is too many miles away to be a reasonable treatment plan option for your client. You also know that this individual is not alone in his or her addiction. Others are suffering as well, and here we find strength. A local church is willing to donate their basement as a meeting space for Alcoholics Anonymous or other similar types of meetings. The strengths here are the church, those interested in starting a program where they can engage in a self-help group, and even you as the social worker who is seeking out the strengths of the community. Further, you find that there are people willing to be sponsors to further the goal of helping others.

Another example can be found in the development of after-school and mentoring programs for youths. All too often rural communities are seen as not being able to adequately provide the education, guidance, and leadership to effectively develop youth leadership and opportunities for growth. Applying a strengths perspective, you may consider developing a program that matches youths with local business leaders, educators, health professionals, and social service providers. The strength of the community is found in the human resources among adults who can and often will quickly embrace this opportunity. In return, the youths receive mentoring and an opportunity to develop knowledge, skills, and abilities that did not otherwise exist. The strengths perspective encourages us to look beyond what we think we see and find opportunities for growth and development that are already there and see the environment as full of possible resources that can be utilized to benefit those living within it.

SOCIAL WORK PRACTICE METHODS FROM A RURAL PERSPECTIVE

From a rural-specific perspective, social work practice methods become much more focused on identifying the needs of others through the processes of help and mutual assistance available in the community. Here it is also important to identify the unique processes that exist in providing high-quality casework at the micro level, shared resources and support at the mezzo level, and the ability for people to band together to address social needs at the macro level. These are identified as and commonly referred to as casework, group work, and community organization.

Casework, Group Work, and Community Organization

Three general practice methods (interventions) are described here as they apply to rural practice: casework, group work, and community organization. These methods are the specific ways in which we work with consumers, families, groups, organizations, and communities. Early in the history of social work as a budding profession, practitioners viewed the field as consisting of only two intervention approaches: casework (with the individual) and group work (with larger groups) (Popple & Leighninger, 2008).

The term *casework* or *micro-level practice* generally refers to the variety of interactions between the social worker and individuals and/or their families. Examples of providing casework include assisting consumers in connecting with social and economic resources and providing therapeutic services and care. From a rural perspective, this can quickly become complicated. For example, you may be one of a few social workers in a community and, as such, are expected to serve consumers in a private, confidential way. Remember, people know each other in rural communities differently than in more urbanized areas. Confidentiality is more difficult to maintain and, to be honest, sometimes nearly impossible. You are driving an individual or family to the grocery store; remember that people recognize you—and them. You are doing good casework by connecting a client with needed services, but you also must remain cognizant of the familiarity aspects of the community.

Group work or *mezzo-level practice* focuses on improving the lives of others through group contact, associations, and processes. This practice method can be conducted to support therapeutic or support groups with the goal of providing care and assistance for others, and consumers to help each other in therapeutic ways. For example, self-help organizations such as Alcoholics Anonymous, Narcotics Anonymous, Al-Anon, Alateen, and other similar groups fall within this domain. But other mezzo-level organizations exist that are more unique to rural areas, such as the National Grange, the Farm Bureau Organization, the National Farm Organization, 4-H, and Future Farmers of America. Yet others are not necessarily limited to rural areas, but hold varying degrees of power and utility in rural places such as fraternal orders such as the Elks, the Eagles, the Independent Order of the Odd Fellows, and the Freemasons. Beyond these national groups, even more state, local, or regional ones exist as well. It's important to understand the power dynamics associated with these groups and how they operate and participate in different rural communities. It is also important to value how these organizations serve communities and how they are able to focus energy and resources.

By the 1930s and partially as a result of the effects of the Great Depression, *community organization* or *macro-level practice* emerged as the third social work practice method. It generally refers to working within and across the broader spectrum of society to improve the quality of life for a large body of people. This practice method includes a vast array of approaches, including organizing communities to address shared concerns and goals, administration, and planning. Historically, this type of work was done through state and national advocacy organizations described earlier (i.e., The Grange, the National Farm Organization). These organizations served as voices from rural regions to government entities, provided opportunities to develop and grow leadership and stewardship, and shaped the form and structure of rural political processes.

These three social work practice methods are effective approaches in the helping process. In the rural context, they can easily become complicated to comprehend and interpret. For example, in more urban areas, one does not need to be as concerned with anonymity between people. In rural areas, we assume that people may know each other at some level. Another concern is that of geographic distance. Casework and group work can be made more complicated when one begins to appreciate the difficulty of logistics across large distances, often referred to as "windshield time," which refers to the amount of time a social worker will spend in the car to deliver services. As one moves more rural, this concern becomes even more challenging. Depending on the location between the worker and the consumer, windshield time can consume several hours traveling to and from meetings, services, and resources. Finally, community organization practice has within it a multitude of concerns as well. Here, we must consider the complexities of local culture, political attitudes, and even religion. To assume that the life ways of rural residents writ large are homogeneous is a mistake and must be avoided.

GENERALIST PRACTICE AND THE GENERALIST INTEGRATION MODEL

Social work as it is interpreted here is generalist in nature and practice. Especially among rural practitioners, generalist practice takes on its own unique meaning when one considers that rural social workers practice more autonomously and often are called upon to provide a wide array of care and services. A generalist practitioner is just that—*a generalist*—meaning, the social worker must be prepared to address a wide variety of concerns across systems, not as a specialist focused on a specific area of concentration (i.e., mental health, gerontology, families, socioeconomic development, community organizing). Here, the social worker is expected to be competent and able to practice effectively across a multitude of situations. Supporting this position, Davenport and Davenport (1995) explain that they believe the generalist model of practice is the model best suited for practicing social work in rural areas. This is largely due to the isolated nature of the geographic space in which the rural social worker practices, which, in turn, leads to lack of available resources and encourages being creative, resourceful, and dynamic. In *Small Town in Mass Society*, Vidich and Bensman (1960) conducted a qualitative study of rural life in an upstate New York community. They found that the life ways of residents in this rural community differed considerably from that found in urbanized areas. The authors explained that in small communities, there is a greater level of independence between people while at the same time a higher level of interdependence on each other. When isolated, people will develop social networks that focus on informal helping systems and develop a sense of identity from locally based norms, needs, and expectations. Supporting this notion, Saltman, Gumpert, Allen-Kelly, and Zubrzycki (2004) investigated unique aspects of rural living, and found "cultural norms of a slower pace of life, importance of informal communication, suspicion of governmental control and outsiders, and the value of independence" (p. 528). Working as a social service provider in rural areas requires the worker to develop an understanding about the local customs and life ways, which often include suspicion toward outsiders, especially those who represent government entities or interests.

Kirst-Ashman and Hull (2001) developed the generalist integration model (GIM), which is characterized by three major features. The first focuses on the definition itself. Generalist social workers are those who assess the consumer's situation and determine the most appropriate course of action to facilitate an effective change strategy (Johnson, 1998). This is accomplished by applying an eclectic base of knowledge, a set of professional ethics and values, and a wide range of skills that can be employed to target systems of any size (Chank & Skovholt, 2006). Here, the generalist practitioner is expected to provide care regardless of the problem or concern. In rural areas, this would include the need to understand the interrelatedness between systems across the spectrum. The second part of the GIM is the specific use of a seven-step planned change method that is flexible enough to meet a variety of needs, and specific enough to effectively guide the user to an appropriate outcome. The seven steps include the following:

- *Engagement.* One must engage in the situation and identify the needs as well as the direction of the intervention focused on creating a positive change.
- *Assessment.* Assess the multiple variables, systems, concerns, and issues to better understand the needs to facilitate change. It is critical to consider as many aspects of the problem or situation as possible so as to effectively move into the next step.
- *Planning.* Develop a plan based on information collected from the assessment process.
- *Implementation.* Implementation of the plan is the action component of the process. Here is where one puts the plan into motion and the actual change event begins to occur.
- *Evaluation.* Once the implementation process has begun, one must begin to evaluate the effectiveness of the planned change event. Special attention should be given to the feedback loop, meaning evaluation information collected must be used to further inform future processes and activities.
- *Termination.* At the point where the implementation process shows effectiveness (through the evaluation process), one must be prepared to terminate the activity that focused on change. When the change has occurred, end the activity.
- *Follow-up.* The follow-up process includes reviewing the outcomes to determine if additional opportunities for change are needed. If this is the case, begin the process starting with the first step again as this is a new change process.

The third feature of the GIM is to orient toward solving problems across multiple levels of interventions, meaning this approach considers micro, mezzo, and macro systems as all targets of change. The use of this model allows the practitioner to analyze nearly all problems across all systems. For example, imagine that you are working toward creating change in a school addressing youth smoking, as youth tobacco use is higher than the national average across many rural communities. At the micro level, you might want to address smoking at the individual level, which may include addressing the needs of addiction through the use of therapeutic interventions, medications, or a combination of both. This can be approached using the seven steps of planned change and is then carefully evaluated, implemented, and measured. The same is true for the mezzo and macro levels as well. By approaching these processes in this way, one can facilitate the planned change process in a thorough, thoughtful, and purposeful way.

CONCLUSION

Social work in rural areas has a long and rich history, but it is filled with a variety of complications, debates, and discussions. Some have argued that practicing social work in isolated areas is no different than in more populated places, pointing out that treatment modalities and therapeutic interventions are essentially applied and practiced the same anywhere. While others generally agree, they also focus more on the nuances, norms, and sociopolitical processes that are unique to rural areas and suggest that how modalities and interventions are applied may be notably different in rural communities. Due to these differences between the two locations, they argue that social work will be practiced differently even if the actual treatment approaches don't differ. Defining what is and isn't "rural" has proved to be problematic to certain degrees. State and federal governments have long worked to define location, some with small differences and some that vary more widely. Others argue that to truly capture the richness and depth of what rural regions fully contain, definitions should include the concept of "perception" as well, as defining rural also includes beliefs, lifestyles, history, culture, and attitudes.

The history of rural social work has vacillated over time between "practicing social work in rural areas" to the more defined practice modality of "rural social work," then back to "practicing in rural areas." This debate is linked to a wide variety of reasons, including how state and federal governments have responded to social needs, the changing socioeconomic processes and demographics of rural areas, and even basic perceptions and misconceptions of rural life.

Understanding theoretical frameworks that assist in formulating responses to rural needs is critical to being an effective rural social worker. While many approaches could be applied, systems and ecological theories are presented as viable ways to better understand conditions, develop responses, and test ideas. In addition, the person-in-environment and strengths perspectives are presented as useful practice models for intervention. Each presents with strengths and weaknesses, and, to effectively practice rural social work, one must be prepared to consider a broader array of theoretical approaches and determine appropriateness based on unique qualities and regional differences.

2

Rural Social Work at the Micro Level
with Carol Goodemann

INTRODUCTION

In this chapter, the provision of rural social work to individuals, couples, and families is explored. The chapter begins with a review of the current literature related to rural context and culture as it relates to social work in micro practice. Next, promising practices identified in the literature for addressing the issues in a rural setting are reviewed. Last, two practice cases highlighting some of the complexities of micro practice are provided.

Social Work Core Competencies Covered in This Chapter:

Competency 1: Demonstrate ethical and professional behavior.

Competency 2: Engage diversity and difference in practice.

Competency 3: Advance human rights and social and economic justice.

Competency 4: Engage in practice-informed research and research-informed practice.

Competency 5: Engage in policy practice.

Competency 6: Engage with individuals, families, groups, organizations, and communities.

Competency 7: Assess with individuals, families, groups, organizations, and communities.

Competency 8: Intervene with individuals, families, groups, organizations, and communities.

Competency 9: Evaluate practice with individuals, families, groups, organizations, and communities.

WHAT IS MICRO-LEVEL SOCIAL WORK PRACTICE IN A RURAL SETTING?

Micro, mezzo, and macro practice in a rural setting have more similarities than differences. The definition of social work practice at the micro level is services provided to individuals, couples, and the nuclear family. The definitions of *couples* and the *nuclear family* are set according to the understanding of the client who is being provided social work services. Micro-level social work practice is provided in all social service, health, and mental health agencies that serve rural areas, both private and public. Practicing social work in a rural area provides both an opportunity and a necessity for developing a range of skills needed to be an effective generalist practitioner. It requires taking on multiple roles as one of the only, or possibly the only, social workers in the community, including building the community's capacity to meet its needs (Humble, Lewis, Scott, & Herzog, 2013). Understanding the community, its history, norms, roles, and traditions, and developing relationships with community members will allow the practitioner to navigate the informal networks needed to work in rural areas (Humble et al., 2013; Lewis et al., 2013). Additionally, rural social workers need to be skilled in identifying and collaborating with agencies and other professionals to make sure individuals, couples, and families receive needed services. Interagency cooperation between institutions within the community and agencies serving the community must occur frequently to ensure scarce resources, both human and monetary, are stretched to reach those in need (Lewis et al., 2013). Human service agencies, hospitals, clinics, schools, mental health agencies, and faith-based service organizations typically employ social workers. Direct practice services may include assessment, prevention, intervention, case management, client advocacy, therapy, referrals, and service coordination.

CURRENT KNOWLEDGE

There is not total agreement in the literature regarding the context and culture of a rural community; however, it provides a starting point for the provision of culturally relevant and evidence-informed micro practice. Although some of the information in the literature may contradict itself, this could be a reflection of the lack of research on rural social work practice. What is known about rural practice is that despite the client system (micro, mezzo, or macro), the methods of addressing issues are interrelated and overlapping.

Rural Context

The first chapter of this book covered rural communities and the context for practice. As social workers consider work with individuals, couples, and families, they need to consider the context in which they are providing services. Rural areas can tend to have residents who are older (Fitzsimons, Hagemeister, & Braun, 2011; Haxton & Boelk, 2010), have an increased risk of substance abuse and mental health issues (Sheridan, 2014), and have an increased likelihood of higher-than-average rates of unemployment and poverty (Henderson & Tickamyer, 2008; Lewis et al., 2013; Slovak, Sparks, & Hall, 2011). Many jobs within rural areas are low paying (Edwards, Torgerson, & Sattem, 2009; Slovak et al., 2011), which results in uninsured or underinsured clients who are unable to receive necessary services (Humble et al., 2013; Stamm, 2003), with high deductibles that must be met to receive needed services. Households often include more than one generation of family members (Humble et al., 2013), increasing the burden of costs on family members. Geographically, populations in rural areas are physically isolated and if effort is not exerted, socially isolated from others (Henderson & Tickamyer, 2008; Slovak et al., 2011). Access to services is hindered by fewer health resources, geographic distance, a lack of transportation (Humble et al., 2013: Mackie & Lips, 2010; Slovak et al., 2011), and an absence of public transportation, such as buses.

Individuals, couples, and families may experience a lack of resources, but problems seeking help are compounded by a lack of mental health and health services in rural areas (Lewis et al., 2013;

Stamm, 2003; Waltman, 2011), including a limited availability of treatment options (Oser, Biebel, Pullen, & Harp, 2011). Even when mental health services are available, they may not be easily accessible, with long waiting lists or little to no available child care (Lewis et al., 2013), and/or the quality of services may not be acceptable (Lewis et al., 2013; Slovak et al., 2011). Perhaps even more concerning, researchers have found that the greater the distance to services, the shorter the length of stay in in-patient treatment and a decreased likelihood of treatment completion (Oser et al., 2011). Additionally, despite the need for coordination of care, there is a lack of coordination among service providers (Stamm, 2003) and resources to provide the care (Humble et al., 2013) that results in a reliance on informal services from family and community members (Humble et al., 2013; Sun, 2011) and a delay in seeking help in a crisis from formal service providers (Sun, 2011).

With the pride and value placed on tradition, and often a resistance to outside services (Humble et al., 2013), comes strong social ties (Humble et al., 2013), the respect for institutions such as schools, churches, clubs, and farming (Edwards et al., 2009; Lewis et al., 2013; Slovak et al., 2011; Sun, 2011; Waltman, 2011, p. 237;), and faith-based traditional and conservative values (Fitzsimons et al., 2011). Attending church activities serves a religious and social purpose (Sun, 2011). Churches and schools are a natural place of gathering within the community and places where community members go to on a regular basis (Lewis et al., 2013). A social worker might find all of these characteristics in a rural culture; however, in moving from one rural community to another, social workers need to understand that there will be differences in the context and culture (Green, 2003) of each community and it is social workers' responsibility to respond to these changes.

Rural America is experiencing an influx of immigrants from nations across the globe (Jensen, 2006). Churches often serve to meet the spiritual, social, and financial needs of rural immigrant populations. However, for non-Christian immigrants, the presence of a faith-based institution is often lacking. One example of this discrepancy in services is provided in a study conducted in a rural community in Minnesota. A survey conducted by the Pew Research

Center's Forum on Religion and Public Life (2010) indicates than over 78 percent of Americans identify as Christian and 0.6 percent identify as Muslims. Shandy and Fennelly (2006) conducted a comparison of Christian and Muslim African immigrants settling in Faribault, Minnesota, a rural community with less than twenty-five thousand residents. The Sudanese Christian population received support from a local Lutheran Church (Shandy & Fennelly, 2006). The immigration experience of the Somali Muslims was less integrative: No informal or formal social structures existed to support them in their acculturation process (Shandy & Fennelly, 2006).

Rural social workers can play a vital role in advocating for sensitivity toward the needs of non-Christian immigrants. Through developing culturally responsive services in meeting the needs of immigrant populations, they can serve as educators for the rest of the community. Understanding the culture will assist in integrating non-Christian populations into rural communities.

Regionalization of Service Delivery

In an effort to address the wide geographic areas that need to be covered in rural portions of a state, agencies have had to colocate (Lewis et al., 2013), consolidate, and regionalize service provision (Haxton & Boelk, 2010). This has been accomplished through collaborations such as shared agency space, use of mobile units, and use of schools and churches after hours and on weekends (Lewis et al., 2013). One social service agency could cover many counties. An example of this might be a private, not-for-profit, mental health agency that provides micro services to individuals, couples, and families. The main office is in a town of sixty thousand and satellite offices are located in twelve surrounding counties. The agency administrator and directors in a central office often do not have a good understanding of the outlying communities (Haxton & Boelk, 2010). Mental health staff attends all meetings, professional development, and/or case conferences at the main office, and then they are physically located in the satellite offices one to two days per week. Clients may drive to the main office to see the social worker or schedule an appointment at the satellite office nearest them on days the office is open (one to two days per week). The length of time for a new patient between the phone call and first appointment can be up to five months. No crisis appointments are available in the office, although they are available in the main office, which could be over two hours away from the satellite offices.

It is easy to see how a rural area can be disadvantaged in both health and mental health care services (Humble et al., 2013; Sun, 2011) in a model such as this. In fact, the main office of the agency has had trouble hiring licensed clinical social workers to fill positions because of the lack of qualified mental health professionals (Humble et al., 2013; Mackie & Lips, 2010; Slovak et al., 2011) in rural areas. Some positions have remained open for over one year, leaving the rural clients with the option of driving to the main office or the closest satellite office. Imagine that not only is there a shortage of mental health professionals, but the local hospital is thirty minutes away, and they, too, cannot fill positions for physicians. The emergency room in the hospital is staffed by physicians who fly in from other states for a few days to meet the staffing need. The closest in-patient mental health unit for adults, if they have an opening, is two hours away. Otherwise, it is located even further away; possibly in a neighboring state. The closest psychiatrist is also two hours away. Clients must rely on their primary care physician for medications (Slovak et al., 2011).

Imagine the challenges of administering a mental health agency that covers such a large geographic area, such as having to manage a budget that must be reduced each year and managing expectations that continue to grow rather than decrease (Mackie & Lips, 2010). Resources in the agency budget must be used to cover mileage for social workers who travel the long distances between offices to see clients and to attend meetings at the main office (Fitzsimons et al., 2011). To overcome challenges and barriers to service in a rural context and culture with a regionalization of services, the focus must be on coordination and/or colocation of services (Humble et al., 2013). Stamm (2003) notes that "the scarcity of workforce resources makes coordination imperative to address service gaps and avoid unnecessary duplication" (p. 9).

PROMISING PRACTICES

Promising practices were identified in the literature for potential transferability into practice. While it might appear that there are many challenges that a social worker must consider when working in a rural community, there are actually many strengths on which to build. These promising practices include utilizing a strengths-based approach when working with clients, identifying informal helping networks to supplement the limited amount of social services available in rural communities, and using an eco-map to help identify informal supports for each client. It is clear from the review of the literature that a generalist approach to social work—utilizing skills at the micro, macro, and mezzo level to address the needs of each client—is effective (Scales & Streeter, 2004). Green (2003) notes that:

> Social workers work across a range of methodologies and intervention strategies. A generalist approach is not only a mode of practice which incorporates different modalities, and requires workers to have the ability to work across different fields of practice, it also includes concepts of interconnectedness, mutuality and reciprocity, interrelatedness and interdependence … not only is a generalist approach appropriate to overcoming the lack of specialist services, it is also most culturally compatible with rural life. (p. 210)

Social workers must be prepared to fulfil multiple roles (Haxton & Boelk, 2010; Humble et al., 2013). In a rural setting, despite utilizing the skills of a generalist social worker, the practitioner is challenged to develop a wide range of skills in specialty areas to address specific client needs when a client cannot access needed services. This forces the development of more advanced clinical skills in a shorter period of time (Green, 2003). As the social worker encounters increasingly complicated situations, it is imperative that he or she remember to practice in his or her areas of competence (Humble et al., 2013). For example, if a client presented with an eating disorder and the social worker does not have the training to treat that eating disorder, he or she would need to refer the client to someone who is trained to work with eating disorders. If the client is not able to travel to someone trained in that area, the social worker could explore providing services under the supervision of someone qualified in that area.

Another example is a social worker who has experience working with adults in a small rural town where there is only one other licensed practitioner in town. The other licensed practitioner specializes in working with children and youths. A couple schedules an appointment to see the social worker, asking her to work with them on parenting their child with autism. They explain that they have contacted the other licensed practitioner, but her caseload is full right now and she is not taking any new patients. The nearest therapist who specializes in working with this population is seventy-five miles away, and the parents do not have a working car. The social worker agrees to see the couple as long as the parents agree to allow the social worker to consult with another social worker who specializes in working with children with autism. The social worker and the couple discuss the pros and cons of this arrangement and agree to review the effectiveness of treatment frequently to ensure the social worker is providing competent services.

In a rural setting, by being creative and having the ability to improvise (Green, 2003), the generalist social worker can meet the needs of the individuals, couples, and families through integrating and coordinating with formal and informal resources (Stamm, 2003). In a rural community payment with goods or services frequently occurs. Lewis et al. (2013) note that "in-kind exchanges . . . [are an] established method of transaction in rural America" (p. 104). Creativity could include using these informal resources to meet the needs of clients. For example, in the absence of child care, a few families could agree to collaborate on child care so that each could work different days. It could also be working with existing stable institutions such as schools and churches, formal and informal service providers, to build the capacity of the community to serve its members by integrating the available limited resources and services (Lewis et al., 2013).

Another promising practice that emerges from the literature review is the use of a strengths-based approach (Martinez-Brawley,

2000) that acknowledges local history, values, traditions, and roles (Green, 2003; Humble et al., 2013; Stamm, 2003), views the community itself as a strength (Haxton & Boelk, 2010; Martinez-Brawley, 2000), utilizes the client(s) as equal partners in care (Haxton & Boelk, 2010), and identifies and builds upon what is already working in the local setting. Haxton and Boelk (2010) state that "a culturally-sensitive and strengths-based approach that stresses finding resources and strategies for problem resolution aimed at helping gain and maintain control is essential" (p. 545). While focusing on micro practice the social worker is building community capacity to meet the needs of that client and others experiencing the same challenges (Humble et al., 2013). One example would be to preserve and strengthen a rural family (Carlton-LeNey, Edwards, & Reid, 1999). Another example is to utilize natural helpers (social support network) and natural-helping networks (Waltman, 2011) within the community. Understanding the community and developing relationships with community members will allow the practitioner to navigate the informal networks needed to work and live in rural areas (Humble et al., 2013). Utilizing the significance of informal helping relationships prevalent in rural areas ensures that social workers have identified all available resources within the community.

Another example of utilizing informal helping networks in the community would be a hospital social worker who works with the Swanson family caring for a thirty-year-old male farmer, Michael, who has broken both legs in a farm accident. Susan, his wife, works full-time in a local factory and is unable to care for her husband during the workday because they are dependent on her income. Susan has no vacation days left because she used them all while her husband was hospitalized. The couple have two children who are ages four and six. Todd, the six-year-old, attends school during the day and James, the four-year-old, goes to daycare. Michael is on the board at a local church and Susan teaches Sunday school. Michael is also an active member of the local Lion's Club. A recently retired neighbor has invited the children over to play and has provided hot meals for the family during Michael's hospitalization. One of Susan's brothers and three of her cousins live in town.

The social worker gathers information about the potential support network to assist the family in planning for the husband's release from the hospital. The hospital social worker engages formal resources in the case: the local home health agency and a public health nurse. The social worker also engages the informal support network (with a written release of information) by contacting the church and Lion's Club and sharing with them the needs of the family. The area farmers support one another and a number of them have started harvesting the family's crops. The social worker encourages Susan to talk with her relatives and neighbor about assisting with the children and other family chores that her husband did when he was able. The literature also emphasized how important it is to know facts about the geographic area, demographics for the context and culture, and all formal and informal community resources in order to put all the issues presented by clients in context (Humble et al., 2013; Scales & Streeter, 2004).

Taught in most social work programs, but not always used in practice, are genograms and eco-maps that can be used as tools to explore context, culture, spirituality, and formal/informal resources with individuals, couples, and families. A genogram is a visual depiction, similar to a family tree, which shows relationships within the family including dates of birth, deaths, illnesses, and other life events (Hepworth, Rooney, Dewberry Rooney, Strom-Gottfried, & Larsen, 2006, p. 209). Patterns such as substance abuse, mental illness, and genetically linked disorders can be revealed across generations (Hepworth et al., 2006, p. 209).

Eco-maps provide a visual tool for reviewing informal and formal sources of support for clients (Ray & Street, 2005) and insight into issues that require further exploration (Ray & Street, 2005). Eco-maps can be utilized to explore "patterns such as social isolation, conflicts, or unresponsive social systems" (Hepworth et al., 2006, p. 232). More detail about an eco-map and an example are provided following the second case application in this chapter.

Spiritual eco-maps are a vehicle for exploring the role of spirituality for the client and additional formal and informal sources of support. The importance of embracing spirituality in the assessment process (Zellmer & Anderson-Meger, 2011) was noted in the literature. The study conducted by Zellmer and Anderson-Meger (2011) concludes that when practitioners explore religious issues with rural residents, it may encourage the individuals to seek professional help. The practitioners need to also remain cognizant of their own spiritual and religious beliefs to ensure those beliefs do not impact their work with rural clients (Zellmer & Anderson-Meger, 2011).

COMMON PRACTICE CHALLENGES AND RESPONSES

Practice issues include professional isolation (Haxton & Boelk, 2010; Humble et al., 2013; Waltman, 2011), a lack of anonymity for both the professional and the client (Edwards et al., 2009; Haxton & Boelk, 2010; Waltman, 2011), challenges to maintaining confidentiality (Humble et al., 2013; Waltman, 2011), and the importance of observing professional boundaries and dealing with not just dual, but multiple, overlapping relationships (Haxton & Boelk, 2010; Humble et al., 2013; Waltman, 2011). This is compounded by the context of service delivery in which the social worker must be a generalist and develop many specialty areas (Humble et al., 2013; Waltman, 2011) through professional development, when accessibility to this training may be an issue, and supervision when there is a lack of qualified professionals in rural areas.

Credibility and community acceptance (Waltman, 2011) is essential to successful work with individuals, couples, and families in a rural setting. The community and specific client(s) must view the social worker as someone who provides a service that is seen as rigorous in the management of personal and private information (Green, 2003; Humble et al., 2013), adheres to ethics (Scales & Streeter, 2004), maintains clarity in the role as a professional (Humble et al., 2013; Waltman, 2011), is competent, and seeks training and supervision (Green, 2003; Haxton & Boelke, 2010) to increase competency. Finally, the use of a rural "reality check" (Dolgoff, Harrington, & Loewenberg, 2012)—ensuring that all ethical choices made in practice are feasible, justifiable, generalizable, and impartial—will ensure the rigor and credibility of practice. Through the application of the Dolgoff, Harrington, and Loewenberg (2012) "reality check," these authors provide an "ethical assessment screen" (p. 61), which assists clinicians with a screening and assessment instrument whereby they can assess their own ethical practice and make sound decisions based on a variety of situations.

EXAMPLE OF A SOLUTION

Imagine that until the age of sixteen you lived in a large metropolitan area in the northeastern United States. You spent much of your time with your five siblings and attended a large high school with two thousand other students in your class. Your mother began selling methamphetamines and was recently incarcerated. You were receiving services from a licensed practitioner to help you cope with the loss of your mother. One day, your father left you and your siblings. You and your siblings are sent to live with an aunt. Your aunt is unable to care for all of the children. You are sent to a small town to live with your grandparents whom you have not seen in years. Your grandparents speak little English, have health problems, and don't drive. You begin getting in fights at school and are frequently suspended. Your grandparents are at a loss as to how to help. With the assistance of the school social worker you and your grandparents are referred for school-based mental health services. Having the opportunity to talk with the mental health care provider at school each week provides an opportunity to process the grief and loss you are experiencing. The fighting subsides and slowly you begin to feel some control over your life. This brief micro case study is one example of the need for mental health services.

A macro solution for a micro issue is the growth of school-based mental health services, which highlights the need for the coordination of existing resources in the community and region. While rural areas tend to have older residents (Fitzsimons et al., 2011; Haxton & Boelk, 2010), children and adolescents residing in these areas need to have specific programming designed to adequately address their mental health concerns. The National Institute of Mental Health projects approximately 20 percent of children aged eight through fifteen either have or will have a serious mental illness sometime during their lives (Merikangas, He, Burstein, Swanson, Avenevoli, Cui,

Benjet, Georgiades, & Swendsen, 2010). Additionally, 11 percent of youths are reported as being severely impaired by a mood disorder, 10 percent severely impaired by a behavior disorder such as attention deficit hyperactivity disorder (ADHD) or conduct disorder, and 8 percent reported as being severely impaired by at least one type of anxiety disorder (Merikangas et al., 2010). The research indicates that 40 percent of the youths also met criteria for at least one other disorder (Merikangas et al., 2010). Identifying youths in need of specialized mental health services does not ensure they will receive the needed treatment. Approximately 36 percent of these youths received mental health services (Merikangas et al., 2010).

Lack of accessible mental health services continues to be a concern of rural practitioners seeking to meet the mental health needs of children, adolescents, and families (Lewis et al., 2013; Stamm, 2003). Offering prevention, intervention, and ongoing counseling within the school setting minimizes the barriers both youths and families face as they attempt to access mental health services. School-employed social workers, counselors, and psychologists provide a safety net for students in need of mental health services. These service providers can meet the basic needs of many in the school population; however, accessing more intensive out-patient services in the community can be difficult due to lack of transportation and availability. Community mental health clinics and schools have developed a solution to this problem by having community mental health agencies send therapists once a week (for example) to see students in the school building. Students with access to school-based mental health services were ten times more likely than students without such access to initiate a visit seeking treatment for mental health issues (Kaplan, Calonge, Guernsey, & Hanrahan, 1998).

Rural schools partnering with local or regional social service agencies, health care providers, and mental health care providers offer rural families easily accessible services (Lewis et al., 2013). Students attend sessions with the mental health care provider at the school, either during school or after school hours, eliminating the need for the student to be transported to a local or regional mental health center. Parents and other community members can receive services at a location that they are most likely to already frequent (Lewis et al., 2013).

Seeking mental health treatment in schools may reduce or eliminate the stigma students and families feel when visiting an unfamiliar service provider (Taras, 2004). This also can apply to a school setting. It is important to eliminate the potential stigma for seeking mental health services within a school setting (Taras, 2004). In small rural schools, students often know most, if not all, of the other students and may question why a student is leaving class and where the student is going. Schools and mental health care providers can help by ensuring as much privacy as possible for the student. This may be accomplished by locating the mental health therapist in an area accessed by students for a myriad of needs, such as meeting with a guidance counselor for college information, signing up for extracurricular activities, or attending meetings with school personnel. Although space in small rural schools is often at a premium, an alternative would be to have a private waiting area and entrance for the students meeting with mental health care providers.

School social workers and counselors often meet with families to discuss how their child's mental health needs may be affecting the academic success of the student. Parents or caregivers are often relieved to learn that their child can access mental health therapy within the school setting. The availability of school-based services ensures that transportation is unnecessary and that the student will not miss some or all of a school day as a result of being transported to an off-site location for services.

The Committee on School Health (2004) states, "In addition to eliminating barriers to access to care, school-based mental health services offer the potential to improve accuracy of diagnosis as well as assessment of progress" (p. 1842). Access to information regarding how a student copes with stress, performs academically, and interacts with peers and adults is all available within the school setting (Committee on School Health, 2004).

PRACTICE APPLICATIONS

The complexity of working in a rural community is highlighted in the case example below. Although the identified client is a middle school student, the parents' issues present themselves and must be addressed in a locally relevant manner according to state-specific laws and the NASW Code of Ethics.

From Tammie Knick, MSW, LICSW

I am a school social worker who has lived and worked in a very rural area for over ten years. The school in which I work has two hundred forty students. The connectedness I feel to this school community is very strong because of the relationships I have established through both my professional and my personal life. I attend church in this community, I volunteer in this community, I socialize in this community, I shop in this community, and I receive health care in this community.

"School Social Worker" is my title or my profession, but my purpose in life is to help improve the lives or situations of others. At times it is difficult to discern between my professional or personal life, as so much of what I do every day, the knowledge and skills I use, underpins all that I am and all that I do. Being a school social worker in a rural area is not always easy. Because of my connectedness in the community, I sometimes find myself in an ethical dilemma caused by dual relationships. In which case, I look to the NASW Code of Ethics for guidance and consult colleagues to ensure I am practicing ethically.

Imagine a well-known community leader coming to my office to discuss concerns about his child's behavior. During our conversation, he discussed his feelings toward his wife whom he was in the process of divorcing. During the conversation, he commented in a threatening manner toward his wife and another well-known community member. After the parent left, I documented our conversation regarding the potential threats. The complexity of this case lies in the fact that this is a well-known person who is connected to me through my school, business, personal, and faith community. It can be difficult to differentiate my role as a school social worker from that as a member of the community where I interact with the individuals involved in an informal manner.

Having to separate my personal life from my professional life is challenging. The two are entwined so closely and dual relationships cross paths frequently. My empathetic character and gut instinct told me the threatening nature of this person's conversation was due to the stress of his family's situation and that he would never follow through with any violent activity. However, due to the nature of the threats, I consulted the NASW Code of Ethics and consultation with a colleague who did not practice in my community and determined that Duty to Warn was evident.

I contacted local law enforcement to report the threatening comments made by this person. The law enforcement officer to whom I reported this situation knows the person well. The officer stated he would like to consult with the county attorney to determine how to proceed. I explained that I would like to meet with the person who made the threatening comments again, along with the law enforcement officer, to determine the intent of his threats and ensure he had a support network and was aware of supportive community resources.

After consulting with the county attorney, the officer asked me to schedule a meeting with the person. During this meeting, the person stated he would never follow through with the threats; rather, he was just angry. I also reported this situation to the school administrators who know the high-profile person well. Throughout this situation, one of the most important things on my mind was how was this situation going to affect the student with whom I work—the one whose father came to see me in the first place.

Later in the week when the student became aware of some of the details of the threats made by her father, she came to my office to ask questions about the situation. Due to confidentiality of the information, I was unable to discuss any details with her, but assured her that I was there to support her, to look out for her best interests, and to help keep her safe. Managing all of the relationships, trying to keep the peace and confidentiality, and continuing to provide service to my client, the student, required a moral and ethical commitment. The knowledge gleaned from research and education was not all that I drew upon throughout this situation. Rather, it was the practice, wisdom, and the personal-social-cultural life experiences that can only come from living and working in a small, rural community. In this case, I was caught off-guard. I had called the parent in to discuss the child's behavior and the conversation changed to focus on the parent's anger and alleged threat toward his spouse and another community member. I should have assessed the severity of the threat with the parent.

ACTIVITIES FOR FURTHER EXPLORATION

1. Create a visual representation of the overlapping roles in this case. What roles might be emphasized more because the social worker is employed in a rural area?
2. Explain how use of the NASW Code of Ethics is visible in this case and how it might differ because it occurs in a rural area.
3. Explore how dual relationships could have impacted this case. Keep in mind the context of a rural setting.

This case provides details on the level of interconnectedness, interrelatedness, and interdependence present in a rural practice setting. It provides a good example of the multiple roles required of a social worker and the importance of high ethical standards for practice. Role clarity was essential to the outcome of this case. The strengths of the rural community and the social worker were important in addressing the issue.

From Carol Goodemann, MSW, LICSW

I am a social worker for a home health agency in a rural Midwest town with a population of 1,503. Everyone in the town knows each other and the most visited place in the town is the corner family-owned restaurant. That is where all the business of the town is informally discussed, relationships made, and decisions considered. The town is very proud of what they have accomplished. They have a drug store that is regionally known for its good service and reasonable prices. They have a news-

paper that is published monthly with all of the local news, including who visited whom for the holidays, who hosted an event in their home and invited whom, and of course, some local news like who got ticketed by the local police. Resources are located in many surrounding towns. While this town has a home health agency and thriving drug store, the nearest hospitals are thirty miles north or east. There is one physician in town and if you are not satisfied with that one, there is a physician two towns over (twenty minutes away) or in the two hospitals (thirty minutes away). The Meals on Wheels program is regionalized and is located about forty minutes away and covers two large counties. Senior housing is available thirty miles away. Public transportation is limited to one, fifteen-passenger van owned by the senior center and reservations are required. There are no buses or other forms of transportation.

One of my clients was an elderly couple who lived just out-side of town. To get to their house, you follow the road out past the Smith's farm and turn right, then turn left at the oak tree; the driveway is the third on the left. The driveway is very steep and two houses sit at the top of the hill. The first house is a big house that the couple vacated years ago so they could live on one level. They also hoped that their favorite niece would move back from the big city to live near them. About three years ago, they deeded their houses and land to their niece so that they could liquidate their assets and apply for Medicaid. One of their neighbors had suggested they do this since this was the only asset they owned.

Normally, my visits with them included a review of all the community agencies working with them and their current needs to ensure that their needs were being met. We also talked about their health conditions and the impact on their ability to care for themselves. They received Meals on Wheels but the driveway to their house was so steep that in the winter, meals would be put in the mailbox. As a result, one of them would have to walk down the steep hill to retrieve them. This could be very challenging but they had a backup plan of calling a neighbor to go get the meals and bring them up if they were unable to do so.

One day when I went to their home, they shared with me that their niece had sold their house and land to a gentleman from the big city. She told them her boyfriend needed the money. They were shocked and very upset because their niece was in an abusive relationship and now they had no idea whether the man who bought the house and land would allow them to continue to live on the property. In fact, they had just received a letter from the new homeowner's lawyer asking them to leave the property.

What Would You Do?

1. How would you apply a strengths-based approach to this case?
2. How might an eco-map help you in your work with the clients?
3. How would you utilize a formal and informal helping network to address the situation?

Application of Eco-Map to Case

As described earlier in the chapter, an eco-map was used as a tool to assist the Swanson family, in identifying the support systems available to them during Michael's recuperation (see fig. 2–1). The direction of the arrows indicates "the direction in which resources flow" (Hartman, 1995; Vodde & Giddings, 2000). Arrows pointing to the circle surrounding the individual family members represent a relationship with the family system. An arrow between an individual and the environmental resource represents the relationship between the family member and the potential resource.

The hospital social worker provides information and resources for the family to help ensure the family's needs are being met. The arrow indicates the worker views his support as strong. The dashed arrow from Michael to the worker provides a visual representation of his stressful relationship with the worker. In a discussion with Michael, he shared that he was uncomfortable needing to receive help and is hesitant to meet with the worker. Michael and his family's involvement with their church is reciprocal with resources flowing both ways. Other strong relationships for all or some of the members of the family system include extended family, Lion's Club, farming community, school, home health care, and daycare center. The neighbor is reaching out to help the family and Michael has said he feels embarrassed that he is unable to help her.

A conflicted relationship exists between Susan and her employer. As discussed in the case study, Susan has used all of her sick leave caring for Michael. Susan has been told she can't miss any more days of work and she is worried that if Michael or one of the children is ill she may need to care for them.

Figure 2-1 Swanson Family Eco-Map

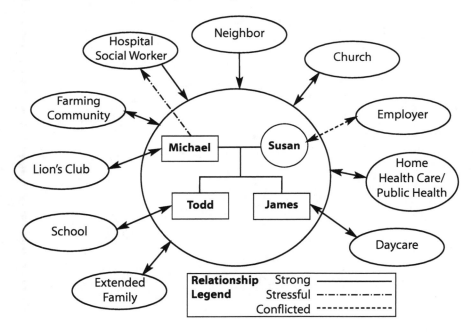

CONCLUSION

This chapter reminds social workers of the reason why understanding the context and culture of a setting can be pivotal in clients obtaining successful outcomes. Utilizing a generalist approach, identifying the need for specialty areas, utilizing a continuum of services developed in collaboration with all local agencies and providers, and practicing in a competent and ethical manner can increase the likelihood that locally relevant and culturally sensitive services are made available to rural communities. Rural social work with individuals, couples, and small groups in a rural area is best summarized by Green (2003) who states, "Where networks are small and multilayered, anonymity, privacy and safety for the social worker cannot be guaranteed, and a broad range of knowledge and skills are demanded" (p. 209).

3

Rural Mezzo Social Work:
Social Work Practice with Groups and Natural Helping Networks

INTRODUCTION

This chapter begins with the conceptualization of mezzo social work practice and establishes a solid foundation of the various modalities within general mezzo-level social work practice. This is followed by a brief historical synopsis of rural mezzo social work practice to help the reader understand the history of the rural context as it relates to mezzo social work practice. Next, a review of the literature is presented that is related to the current knowledge and promising practices in rural mezzo social work practice. Common practice challenges frequently encountered in rural mezzo practice are identified along with possible responses to help mitigate these challenges. Finally, this chapter concludes with resources related to mezzo-level practice.

Social Work Core Competencies Covered in This Chapter

Competency 1: Demonstrate ethical and professional behavior.

Competency 2: Engage diversity and difference in practice.

Competency 3: Advance human rights and social and economic justice.

Competency 4: Engage in practice-informed research and research-informed practice.

Competency 5: Engage in policy practice.

Competency 6: Engage with individuals, families, groups, organizations, and communities.

Competency 7: Assess with individuals, families, groups, organizations, and communities.

Competency 8: Intervene with individuals, families, groups, organizations, and communities.

Competency 9: Evaluate practice with individuals, families, groups, organizations, and communities.

WHAT IS MEZZO SOCIAL WORK PRACTICE IN A RURAL SETTING?

Prior to examining the nuances of mezzo social work practice in a rural setting, it is essential that we establish a solid foundation of the various modalities that exist within general mezzo-level social work practice. Generally speaking, mezzo social work practice focuses on improving the lives of others through mobilizing extended family systems, facilitating various types of groups, and connecting with existing natural helping networks.

Extended Family Systems. Mobilizing needed resources for client systems is the cornerstone of all social work practice and begins with examining social supports available within the family and extended family systems. Due to the current economic recession and other sociopolitical trends (delayed age of first marriage, increased life expectancy, and immigration into this country), multigenerational families are on the rise. A multigenerational family consists of three or more generations living in the same household. According to the 2010 Census Brief, multigenerational households have increased by 30.8 percent from 3.9 million multigenerational households in 2000 to 5.1 million in 2010 (Lofquist, Lugaila, O'Connell, & Feliz, 2012). This trend of the nuclear and extended families living together to make ends meet during tough economic times makes social work practice with large family systems more commonplace. This will require social workers to have knowledge of family systems theory, as well as understanding the dynamics and processes of working with groups. We would be remiss if we did not remind social workers to be cognizant that not all extended family members are blood related or related through marriage. Families often create fictive kinship networks. These are networks of people whom the family have identified as family, such as an aunt or uncle who is not related through blood or marriage, but who the family has identified as family. Social workers need to be mindful of language choice when discussing the family and extended family and allow the client system to define what constitutes family or extended family to them. For example, it's not uncommon for relatives who may be extended family members (or not biologically related at all) to be referred to as "aunt" or "uncle" based on social or familiar contact or resource connectedness. Further, some cultures and regions will refer to close friends or others who are seen as a part of the community as "cousin," "brother," or "sister."

Various Types of Groups. As social workers begin to practice with larger family constellations that include extended family members, understanding group dynamics and processes becomes critical. Group work is defined as a "goal directed activity that brings together people for a common purpose or goal" (Toseland & Horton, 2008, p. 298). Group work is practiced in all social work settings to varying degrees. The nature of the group work is highly dependent on the type of group being convened. Toseland and Rivas (2012) provide a classification of the various types of groups that distinguishes natural from formed groups and treatment from task-oriented groups.

"Natural groups come together spontaneously on the basis of naturally occurring events, interpersonal attraction, or the mutually perceived needs of members" (Toseland & Rivas, 2012, p. 13). These groups are often informal and have a longer developmental history. This developmental history has implications for practice as social workers need to be aware of the shared history among group members and the cultural dynamics of the group. We will cover natural groups more in depth later in this chapter when we discuss natural helping networks. Natural groups can include family groups, peer groups, friendship networks, street gangs, cliques, neighbors, and special interest clubs. Formed groups, on the other hand, are those groups that come together through the deliberate actions of the group leader to offer some type of intervention. These groups are convened for a particular purpose and the group leader decides group membership. Formed groups can include treatment and task-oriented groups.

The purpose of treatment groups is to meet members' "socio-emotional needs" (Hepworth, Rooney, Rooney, & Strom-Gottfried, 2013, p. 296) and achieve individual members' personal goals. Treatment groups are characterized by open communication and interaction among members, procedures that range from flexible to formal (depending on the group), and high levels of self-disclosure; proceedings are kept confidential; and evaluation is based on meeting individual members' treatment goals (Toseland & Rivas, 2012).

Toseland and Rivas (2012) propose six treatment group subtypes—support groups, education groups, growth groups, therapy groups, socialization groups, and self-help groups. They characterize these treatment group subtypes by their unique purposes. Support groups strive to assist members with stressful life events and focus on increasing coping skills (e.g., a loss survivors' group). Education groups center on helping members to learn new information and skills (e.g., birthing classes for expectant mothers, health groups for adolescents). Growth groups help members develop awareness and insight about themselves and others (e.g., sexuality groups for questioning youths, empowerment groups for women). Therapy groups help members change behaviors and resolve personal problems (e.g., psychotherapy groups for clients, chemical dependency groups). Socialization groups help members to learn social skills and offer opportunities to practice social skills (e.g., social skills groups for youths with pervasive developmental delays or disruptive behavior disorders). Self-help groups may share characteristics with support, educational, and socialization groups, but the distinguishing characteristics are that these groups are led by members who share the problem experienced by the group members (e.g., Alcohol Anonymous and Narcotics Anonymous).

Task groups, on the other hand, are established to accomplish or carry out a task. These groups are frequently used in agencies and organizations. They are characterized by communication focused on the task to be accomplished, procedures that are formal and predicated by an agenda or rules, low levels of self-disclosure, proceedings that may be private or public, and evaluations based on accomplishing the task or producing a product (Toseland & Rivas, 2012). Toseland and Rivas have identified three primary purposes of task groups. They are: (1) meeting client needs (teams, treatment conferences, and staff development), (2) meeting organizational needs (committees, cabinets, and boards of directors), and (3) meeting community needs (social action groups, coalitions, and delegate councils).

Natural Helping Networks. Natural helping networks are natural groups, as described in the previous section. These natural helping networks, while not distinctly a rural phenomenon, are often the lifeblood of rural and small communities. Historically, rural communities have had to develop a greater sense of mutuality and reliance on one another, as many of these communities were oftentimes geographically isolated from larger towns or cities and resources were scarce for these agriculturally dependent communities. Neighbors borrowed goods and equipment from each other and helped one another in times of need. This culture of sharing resources and "taking care of their own through informal mechanisms" has become a rural way of life (Watkins, 2004, p. 66). This reliance on natural helping networks may foster a reluctance to utilize more formal helping networks offered by social service and mental health agencies (Jacob, Willits, & Jensen, 1996).

Natural helping networks can exist anywhere in a rural community. These networks can range from an informal structure (e.g., the group of farmers' wives who regularly meets for social time, the group of older men who meets to have coffee every Tuesday morning at the local café, or the group of youths who meet frequently at the pizzeria) to a more formal structure (e.g., the women's group from the local church, the group of men who regularly meets at the Veterans of Foreign Wars (VFW) or the Moose Lodge, or the youths who participate in 4-H, Boy Scouts, or the Girl Scouts). These groups are not developed or implemented by a group leader. Rural social workers need to be knowledgeable about these existing natural groups as a potential resource to link client systems. This means that the rural social worker must know the community in which he or she works and develop relationships and social capital within these communities. There are obvious ethical practice implications (e.g., confidentiality and releases of information) that need to be flushed out when linking a client system to an existing natural group; this will be covered in the practice challenges section at the end of this chapter.

We mentioned in the previous section that natural helping networks have a longer developmental history; this requires more elaboration to clearly understand the potential practice implications that exist. In rural and small communities, "relationships are characteristically face-to-face because association is composed of primary, family-like groups" (Ginsberg, 2005, p. 6). This close proximity that is created by the small town atmosphere in geographically isolated communities increases the intensity of interaction between community members. This creates more frequent exchanges between community members, thus fostering a sense of trust between them and increasing the likelihood that community members are aware of other community members' problems (Gumpert & Saltman, 1998). This intensity in interaction can also create severed bonds between community members due to some type of disagreement or perceived breaches of trust, much like the Hatfield–McCoy feud, albeit more civilized.

Understanding the potential for a longer developmental history among natural groups in small and rural communities stresses the need for social workers to have honed their basic generalist social work practitioner skills, particularly understanding the importance of the person in environment perspective, as discussed in the introductory chapter. Social workers will need to assess the rural and small communities that they work in and try to become accepted and trusted by the rural community. This requires building relationships and engaging the community as one of its devoted members. This vantage point will allow for the transmission of knowledge about the community's cultural and value system, as well as the knowledge of and history of existing natural helping networks.

HISTORY OF RURAL MEZZO SOCIAL WORK PRACTICE

The history of rural mezzo social work practice (practice with extended families, groups, and natural helping networks) is not widely documented in the literature. The 1933 seminal rural social work text, *The Rural Community and Social Case Work*, by Josephine Brown documents the cultural structure of rural communities and provides practical knowledge for rural social workers, much of which holds true for contemporary rural social work practice. Her emphasis is on the rural family and casework but does acknowledge the role of collateral sources of information necessary to work with families. Many of these collateral sources are in fact facets of existing natural helping networks, such as neighbors, employers, teachers, and clergy (Brown, 1933).

Although she does not specifically discuss treatment groups, Brown does elaborate on the importance of group work related to networking with and educating existing resources and community groups. She identifies the importance of attending various community club meetings (e.g., Kiwanis Club), regional conferences, holding neighborhood/community meetings, attending countywide township meetings, and providing educational talks to school students (Brown, 1933). She stresses the importance of knowing the community and the available resources and "joining" with these natural groups to form relationships that will be required to address various client systems' needs. Joining with existing natural groups requires the development of a relationship and the requisite level of trust, thus much of the time the mezzo-level social worker will be engaging others and establishing a solid foundation of rapport with key stakeholders of the community.

Furthermore, the cultural context of rural communities has remained relatively static throughout history, placing emphasis on the values of mutual assistance (Watkins, 2004) and informal support systems (Riebschleger, 2007), strong faith with community religious institutions (Ginsberg, 2005; Meystedt, 1984; Waltman, 1986; Watkins, 2004), and traditions (Waltman, 1986; Zapf, 2009). Understanding the cultural context and associated values of rural communities is imperative for equipping social workers to practice effectively at the mezzo level. For instance, the literature suggests that there is a "dearth" of formal resources in rural communities (Riebschleger, 2007, p. 204). This lack of formal resources can be augmented by the savvy rural social worker who is well connected to the existing natural helping networks in the community. This includes tapping into existing natural groups and resources available from the local religious institutions. Additionally, rural social workers need to understand the traditions and seasonal and social rhythms of the community, such as harvest periods, game patterns, local festivals, and celebrations (Zapf, 2009). In many rural and small communities, the citizens get together to celebrate their community's political, economic, or cultural heritage (i.e., Marquette, Michigan, and Finn Fest; Nevis, Minnesota, and Muskie Days; Girdwood, Alaska, and the Fungus Fair). These events create implications for mezzo-level social work practice that will be discussed in the practice challenges section, but they also provide opportunities to "join" with the community. In fact, these are often the best places for a rural social worker to connect with communities they represent and residents they seek to assist. These are also places where trust and interpersonal relationships can be solidified as evidence of people's commitments to each other and to common beliefs and attitudes.

Rural Mezzo Fields of Practice

Mezzo-level social work practice can occur across nearly all fields of practice, especially in rural areas where even if a practitioner is "specific" in their training, education, and skills, they are often expected to practice in a more generalized style. Below, we specify fields of practice that are more suited for mezzo-level interventions, with the understanding that group work is something that can occur across a variety of areas.

School Social Work. School social workers are deeply involved in the lives of children and youths, which nearly always include the extended family members and the surrounding community. Rural schools are often one of the few places where children and youths can readily access mental health and social services and do so with a certain amount of anonymity.

Family Services. Family service and child welfare workers are those who work with children and families, often at the mezzo level, and seek to develop appropriate responses to family needs. In rural areas, obtaining resources for families can be especially difficult due to effects of geographic isolation, distance between resource points, and poverty.

Health Care. Rural hospitals and clinics are often the only place where individuals can readily access health care and mental health care. Social workers can develop and maintain a variety of services that are based with these service providers.

Alcohol and Other Drug (AOD) Treatment. Rural areas are just as susceptible to challenges associated with addictions as found in more populated areas. However, rural areas often lack immediate access to treatment centers and are more dependent on natural helping systems such as Alcoholics Anonymous (AA), Narcotics Anonymous (NA), and other group-based helping services.

Mental Health. Not unlike more populated areas, rural residents experience mental illness. However, in rural areas, services are typically less accessible and after- or follow-up care less formal. For those receiving mental health care, the need to identify natural helpers or groups to assist in the care of others becomes critical and is a common process.

Administration and Management. All social service agencies need high quality, competent, and caring leadership—and those located in rural areas are no different. At the mezzo level, rural agencies are places where social workers often work more independently with fewer supports and resources. Due to these unique challenges, rural agencies need skilled administrators who understand group dynamics, rural culture, and how these elements intersect with each other.

CURRENT KNOWLEDGE

Upon reviewing the literature specific to rural mezzo-level social work practice, it became abundantly clear that this is an underdeveloped topic in the rural literature. Despite the growth in group work, a response to agencies downsizing and managed care, the literature focused on rural group work is at best in its infancy (Gumpert & Saltman, 1998). Most of the literature on social work with groups is centered on an urban context, which does not address the rural cultural nuances that exist and affect group work, such as instances where the group leader and group members know and regularly encounter each other outside of group (Zapf, 2009). The literature suggests that group work is one of the least used modalities by rural generalist social work practitioners, as compared to individual and family modalities (Gumpert & Saltman, 1998). This may be linked to some of the practice implications common to practicing in rural and small communities that will be expanded on in the practice challenges section of this chapter, such as traveling long distances, fearing stigma, not having enough group members, and lack of anonymity.

The limited literature on mezzo-level social work practice, specifically the group work modality, suggests that social work practitioners should consider moving away from "a narrowly defined group practice model which focuses exclusively on clinical assessment of individual members" and "makes minimal use of the group as the means of help" (Gumpert, 1985, p. 50). Gumpert suggests utilizing a broader group framework, such as the Mainstream Model of Social Work with Groups developed by Papell and Rothman, which emphasizes a systemic approach to group work that taps into existing natural helping networks and rural culture as avenues for therapeutic intervention. This model acknowledges the interaction among the individual group members, the group as a whole, and the environment of the group, thus providing rural social workers with a framework for deliberately assessing "the realities of rural life, the influence of cultural norms and values, and the dynamic interaction on several levels of community life in the thoughtful process of planning and implementing a group service" (p. 52).

Additionally, there is some literature that has focused on specific group work approaches and group work with specific populations. Literature specific to the development of support groups in a rural context includes: developing a support group with homicide survivors (Blakley & Mehr, 2008); developing a support group for families and partners of people with HIV/AIDS (Anderson & Shaw, 1994); and developing a support group for female survivors of domestic violence (Andrews, 1987). Literature specific to the use of telephone groups in a rural context includes: linking people with AIDS (Rounds, Galinsky, & Stevens, 1991); an overview of telephone group work (Toseland, 2009); and telephone technology in group treatment (Mallon & Houtstra, 2007). Literature specific to rural group work with children includes: group intervention with children (Lane & Judd, 1990) and group therapy with male children with acting out behaviors (Swerdlik, Rice, & Larson, 1978).

Although some of this literature is older, it does provide a starting point for rural social work practitioners when developing similar groups with similar populations. Unfortunately, this literature is narrowly focused on specific group work issues and may be of little help to rural social work practitioners looking to engage in other group work approaches or with other populations. This emphasizes the need for rural social work practitioners to contribute to the rural mezzo social work knowledge base by publishing their group work, and for those intimidated by this suggestion to consider collaborating with social work faculty at local colleges and universities.

PROMISING PRACTICES

Telephone Groups. Despite some of the limitations with the existing literature, there are some promising practices embedded that will be of benefit to the rural mezzo-level social worker. First, the literature supports the use of telephone groups in rural and small communities, especially in instances where stigma may be attached to the individual group members or geographic distances make it difficult to attend. A quick word of caution: although the current research supports using telephone groups for support and educational groups, additional research is needed to determine the effectiveness of using telephone groups to convene therapy groups.

Rounds, Galinsky, and Stevens (1991) implemented a support group that linked people with AIDS in rural communities. They found that support groups for people with AIDS were not accessible to rural residents because of geographic distances between potential group members, lack of or limited transportation resources, and being fearful of the stigma and the lack of anonymity. This parallels Gumpert's (1985) premise that it may be difficult to recruit group members for specific face-to-face groups (i.e., support group for people with HIV) due to the sparse number of people experiencing the same issue within one rural or small community. Telephone groups are an innovative approach that overcomes geographic distances, reduces isolation, increases mutual support, and ensures confidentiality. The literature also suggests that group development and process is not negatively affected by this technological innovation (Mallon & Houtstra, 2007), but that group facilitators must take "a more active role in the interaction processes between members" because members cannot see each other so there are no visual cues and also to help members know who is speaking (Toseland, 2009, p. 315).

There are a couple of noted limitations to using telephone groups. First, there may be a cost in providing the service as special teleconferencing equipment may be needed. However, with the technological advances available through the Internet, such as various voice-over-Internet protocol (VOIP) services (i.e., Skype), the costs have significantly decreased (Toseland, 2009). Also, using VOIPs does not necessarily require the group members to have a computer or Internet access as they can still receive their calls on standard telephone equipment. With advancing technology and increased affordability of computers, convening such groups over the Internet may also be worth investing in. The social worker will need to be properly trained to use such equipment and must ensure the client's confidentiality will not be breached. Finally, rural social workers interested in developing a telephone group need to check into reimbursement requirements for such services in their state.

Self-Help and Support Groups. Another promising practice that surfaced in the literature related to mezzo-level social work practice was the feasibility of using self-help, support groups or other groups that were more broad and less focused on the medical model. These groups appear to be more commonly practiced in rural communities and are more widely accepted within the culture of rural communities (Gumpert & Saltman, 1998). This suggests that specialized therapy groups may not be the best fit in rural communities for a number of reasons. First, as previously discussed, there may not be enough individuals in the rural/small community experiencing the same specialized issue, such as a dialectical behavior therapy (DBT) for persons with bipolar disorder, to generate sufficient group recruitment (Gumpert, 1985).

Second, there is a lack of anonymity in rural and small communities. Simply parking your car in front of a mental health or social service agency implies to those who pass by and recognize your vehicle that you receive services at that agency. This "life in a goldfish bowl" is a common rural phenomenon (Davenport & Davenport, 2008). This may contribute to the resistance to formal helping systems in rural and small communities for fear of becoming part of the gossip mill. Fear of the gossip mill may make group members hesitant to expose personal problems in a group setting (Gumpert, 1986).

Third, there is often a longer developmental history between individuals in rural communities due to the intensity in interaction that can create varying levels of trust depending on the nature of the shared history. This can hinder group development, which is essential for effective therapy groups. For instance, if individuals have had a long-standing family feud, then the group may never progress with the requisite level of trust to advance to a working stage. On the other hand, if members in a group share a high level of trust they propel the group into the transition or working stage prematurely. This could cause other group members to withdraw from the group or to terminate services.

Finally, rural life is informal and personal (Ginsberg, 2004; Gumpert, 1985). This lack of formality may be more conducive to more broad group topics (i.e., self-esteem, caregivers support, stress management) and to support and educational groups. Support and educational groups bolster the rural community tradition of mutual support. Keeping group topics broad and that fit in with the community's unwritten moral code will garner community support for the group and decrease any potential related stigma for attending.

COMMON PRACTICE CHALLENGES AND RESPONSES

Several common practice challenges and effective responses are identified and addressed in the mezzo level of social work practice in rural areas. One of the first and most important issues is that of geography—the sheer reality of how distant people can be from needed resources. To address this as a concern, opportunities now exist using technology as simple as a telephone or as complex as the Internet and audiovisual software. Today, groups of people can connect in ways not possible (or affordably feasible) even a few years ago. Telephones can now be used to communicate across a number of people at the same time. Audiovisual technology now allows groups to interact visually and, thus, more personally. The use of these processes in turn can bridge the gaps in groups created by the isolation often associated with rural areas. Closely related, natural helping networks can become enhanced through the use of technology in group settings. Natural helpers can be utilized to assist and support others, and do so in a more informal manner.

The use of technology allows for closer relations, which may in turn create opportunities that increase the phases of group development but, at the same time, could also impede the process. When people are comfortable with the use of technology and understand both the opportunities and the limitations, group development can be enhanced. When people do not have these skills, the use of technology may impede the ability to have gainful benefits from the use of these processes.

There are obvious ethical practice implications associated with the use of technology in group or mezzo care environments. Perhaps most important are concerns raised regarding confidentiality and access to information. In any group environment, the possibility of violating confidentiality must be addressed and proper precautions made. In the use of technology, there is even a greater opportunity for confidentiality to be compromised through the use of unsecure computers, phones, or networks. While the likelihood of violating confidentiality has been reduced through the application of better security systems, the possibility of unauthorized access still remains a very real concern. Specifically in rural areas, the lack of anonymity must be assumed, especially in areas where even if the geography is large, the population may be small. In places such as this, it is not uncommon to find people who know each other or know of each other even across large distances. The rural social worker engaged in mezzo practice has to remain constantly mindful that in rural areas, people have a tendency to have lived in the area for a considerable amount of time, are familiar with people and surnames, and likely even know each other at some level. Here is where following proper protocols and ethical practices is paramount to the success of a group. Specifically, there is a need to maintain good order on release of information, and when developing a helping group, carefully seek to identify potential conflicts of interest and violations of confidentiality. This is especially important to address when one is linking a new person to an existing natural helping network or group. The social worker needs to have fully considered the possibilities of connectedness between those in the group and the person entering into the relationship (Davenport & Davenport, 2008). Finally, currently there is a notable lack of research on rural group work. Other areas of rural practice (e.g., micro and macro) have been better studied and findings disseminated. It is well recognized that those living in rural areas can benefit from group therapeutic relationships no differently than in more populated areas, but how to best go about doing this in rural areas has yet to be well defined.

PRACTICE APPLICATIONS

Rural Group Case Study

From Tom McNeely, MSW, LICSW

My introduction to rural group work occurred in a small town in southern Missouri. I was in the process of completing an internship and had been attending dialectic behavior therapy training and cofacilitating a group in the larger community for

*approximately a year. I was relatively confident in my new skills
and a bit full of myself when I agreed to travel one day per week
to this rural clinic to provide a group for a small number of
clients who, at the time, were not responding well to services currently offered. My internship supervisor also worked in this clinic
setting full-time, so it provided an opportunity to meet with him
regularly. The agency lacked the resources to staff the group per
DBT model standards, meaning that I did not have a cofacilitator.*

*The individual members of the group were transferred to my
caseload, as I had been advertised as having the training and expertise needed to work effectively with them. Some members were
not pleased with this arrangement and others were thrilled, but
in both instances I had no idea what I was about to undertake.*

*I held individual sessions with each prospective client and
introduced the treatment model and an overview of the process. I
obtained consent and had each person sign a "commitment statement" that essentially was an agreement saying that they would
attend all sessions and complete assigned homework, including a
diary card. It was during this process that I discovered there
were going to be challenges I had not considered when volunteer-
ing to provide therapy in this setting.*

*Significant unsolicited information was provided to me dur-
ing these initial meetings. Information like, "I am not coming to
this group if 'so and so' is going to be there; I hate that bitch."
After discussion with the only licensed therapist in the clinic I
learned that this person and her disliked peer had been attending
one type of group or another for many years. They were on-again,
off-again friends who were sensitive, competitive, and jealous of
one another, particularly related to their therapy providers,
which they had also had to share for years.*

*Additionally, I heard things like, "I will only come if the group
(and individual sessions) were held in the evening" because the
clinic was along a busy street (by busy I mean this street had the
town's only flashing red light) and the person was concerned that
"everyone" would see his or her car in front of the "shop for crazy
people."*

I also soon discovered that the sweet middle-aged "clinic coordinator" was actually a bit of a dictator. She had been with the agency for many years, longer than about anyone in the organization. She had seen clinicians come and go, but in this clinic she ran the show how she saw fit. In her mind the administration's policy and procedure manual was more of a reference than an expectation. She knew everyone within a twenty-five-mile radius and was likely related to most of them in one way or another. One of the prospective group members was the daughter of her close friend, and she felt obliged to provide the client's backstory in the waiting area of the clinic. She greeted clients in an overly familiar manner, which caused me to feel uncomfortable but to my surprise didn't seem to bother the clients that much. This observation made it a bit tricky to address because I didn't have an obvious situation to point to when addressing the problem with this mode of operation. However, with some examples of how this might violate confidentiality, she reluctantly agreed to "tone it down" and, for the most part, she did—at least in my presence.

After some redirection, smooth talking, and negotiation, I had six clients who agreed to attend the group and committed to the model's attendance agreement—including both the person who said she would not attend if a certain other person was going to attend and the person to whom she was referring. For the first few weeks, things seemed to be going relatively well. There was significant confusion related to the material, but everyone respected the group rules they helped create during the first session and a couple of the members were really motivated. At this point, however, a couple of the members began to target another group member with dismissive looks or would make subtle, negative comments when she shared information about her weekly goals or skills usage. Over the course of the next few weeks, it became known that the two members teaming up against this client were going out for coffee or lunch every week after the group and discussing what other members were doing or not doing. I did not hear of them discussing information with nongroup members, but it was apparent that these meetings were affecting the group dynamics. Despite addressing the issue with them both during individual sessions and their discontinuing the meetings after group sessions, the behavior did not cease completely. Eventually one of the two was suspended from the group. This change contributed positively to the group as a whole as well as to the other individuals' engagement in the therapy.

LEARNING ACTIVITIES AND DISCUSSION POINTS

Based on the information provided above, please consider responding to the following learning activities and discussion points:

1. How might a social worker assist clients with concerns about confidentiality and being identified as someone receiving services?
2. How might social workers develop group membership, where members work well together and the group is therapeutically beneficial, and, at the same time, maintain confidentiality?
3. How could the social worker in the case study better work with the clinical coordinator whom he felt shared too much information about clients with others?

CONCLUSION

Social work practice is well grounded in the use of groups and natural helpers to achieve therapeutic benefits for clients. While often practiced in our field, we understand that group processes have the real potential to operate differently in rural areas. At the moment one brings people together in a group setting, anonymity is immediately breached. In a more populated area, confidentiality can be protected by bringing group members together from different neighborhoods or communities, knowing that the likelihood of them knowing each other is low. In rural areas, people often know or at least know of each other across a large geographic space. This creates the potential for conflict as the social worker tries to create a group that is beneficial while, at the same time, safe. How one goes about doing this can be challenging, but, as noted in this chapter, not impossible. The social worker must be more astute to the identities and needs of the group members and be more cautious about how therapeutic groups are formed. It is critical that group members be educated about the need to maintain confidentiality and respect for each other and see that the most important facet of being a part of the group is for all participants to become stronger, healthier, and more successful in their treatment.

Related Websites and Other Resources (for Further Learning Opportunities, Discussion Questions):

- The Association for the Advancement of Social Work with Groups, Inc. (AASWG), an international professional organization, is the premier international association for social workers and allied helping professionals engaged in group work. http://www.aaswg.org/about-aaswg
- *Social Work with Groups* is a journal about group work but not specifically rural focused.
- *Contemporary Rural Social Work*, a collaboration between the National Rural Social Work Caucus and The Center for Rural Education and Communities in the College of Education and Human Development at the University of North Dakota.

4

Rural Social Work at the Macro Level

INTRODUCTION

Social work practice from a macro perspective is a large, broadly encompassing array of multifaceted responses to social, economic, and political challenges and opportunities in communities. Rural social workers face a multitude of complex issues ranging from needing to organize people to advocate for the betterment of their communities to working toward influencing political entities to provide assistance and support to improve the lives of constituents. In this chapter, concepts associated with what rural social work macro practice is (and isn't), the state of current knowledge and promising practices, and common practice challenges are addressed.

Social Work Core Competencies Covered in This Chapter:

Competency 1: Demonstrate ethical and professional behavior.

Competency 2: Engage diversity and difference in practice.

Competency 3: Advance human rights and social and economic justice.

Competency 4: Engage in practice-informed research and research-informed practice.

Competency 5: Engage in policy practice.

Competency 6: Engage with individuals, families, groups, organizations, and communities.

Competency 7: Assess with individuals, families, groups,
            organizations, and communities.
Competency 8: Intervene with individuals, families, groups,
            organizations, and communities.
Competency 9: Evaluate practice with individuals, families,
            groups, organizations, and communities.

WHAT IS MACRO PRACTICE IN A RURAL SETTING?

Defining Macro Practice from a Rural Perspective

What is macro social work practice? Answering this question
may be more difficult than one might initially think. Practicing social
work in the macro context is sometimes called practicing
"indirectly," meaning, not directly with clients but instead with
systems that support individuals, families, groups, communities, and
societies. Macro practice is many different things to many different
people. Community organizing, regional planning, advocacy, policy
and political work, leadership, supervision, and administration are
all examples of macro social work practice. From a rural practice
perspective, understanding the importance of macro practice is
critical to the helping process. While it is important to understand
micro practice processes, often assisting with needs within the macro
environment is where we do our best work. Rural areas are,
of course, defined by their geographic location, and within these
locations there is considerable evidence of differences from urban
areas. Rural areas at large tend to show lower median household
incomes, have higher rates of illness, and have lower levels of health
care when compared to urban areas (Ricketts, 1999). In addition,
access to child, maternal, and prenatal health care services is lower,
as is access to mental health care. Disparities in access to care and
services increase when one considers special populations such as
children, the elderly, the gay community, and ethnicities other than
European heritage. While these population concerns are addressed
through micro systems of care, the greater issues can and should be
addressed from the macro system. For the purposes of this book, four
main macro social work areas will be discussed in the rural context;

community organizing, economic development, policy formulation, and legislative action.

In rural and small communities, core concepts continue to be important but may manifest differently from what one might find in more populated areas. For example, rural areas show greater levels of poverty among the population compared to urban areas (Ulrich, 2010). We also know that poverty contributes to a variety of social problems, including challenges associated with adequately funding and supporting infrastructure such as schools, roads, businesses, and government services (Mackie, 2012). Based on this knowledge, it is reasonable to believe that rural social workers have a responsibility to work in the macro realm and focus on developing strategies to improve the quality of life for rural residents from a policy and communities position. To do so, perhaps it's best to begin with an understanding of the historical aspects of rural macro practice, as rural areas are often grounded in different ideologies, attitudes, beliefs, and perceptions when compared to more populated areas.

HISTORICAL ASPECTS OF MACRO PRACTICE

Historically, the field of social work essentially began in the macro environment. For example, the work of Jane Addams through the Settlement House focused on improving living conditions among the Chicago poor. A focus on improving working and living conditions, access to basic necessities, and responding to the needs of communities writ large are all examples of macro practice. From a rural perspective, the history of macro social work practice is similar in focus, but looks different.

Rural social work generally defined was discussed in Chapter 1 of this book. Specific to the history of macro social work practice, definitions are more difficult to establish. Macro practice social work in rural areas is essentially how rural social work was originally perceived—macro preceded micro. Historically, macro practice was "the" defined way in which rural practice was typically defined and conducted. Early on in the United States, rural social work practice focused almost exclusively on addressing the economics and politics of a largely agrarian (agricultural-based) society. It focused on the development of agricultural skills, home economics, economic development, and community as well as personal hygiene. As one sees, there was little in the way of what social work looks like today. This was largely a utilitarian response to rural needs; those living in rural and remote areas were viewed as needing to be prepared for rural life.

FIELDS OF RURAL MACRO PRACTICE

The fields of macro social work practice are vast and often difficult to define. The rural social worker will have opportunities to work in agencies that focus on providing general social services, educational assistance, and policy development and implementation. Specifically, the following fields are important areas of social work practice in rural areas:

- *Community organizing.* Nearly always remote and too often, lacking similar access to services found in more populated areas, residents of rural areas are excellent resources to identify social, economic, and political needs. A well-prepared social worker can be an important and critical participant in the process of mobilizing forces and resources to successfully advocate for services or assist in the development of grassroots activities focused on planned, positive change. In this capacity, the social worker serves as an organizer and an advocate.
- *Community organisation/community development.* Sometimes confused with "community organizing," community organization focuses on organizing social structures and systems within a community to facilitate positive change. Social workers are uniquely poised to work with stakeholders to strengthen communities and bring different constituents together to develop successful strategies to build a stronger community. In this capacity, the social worker serves as an organizer, planner, or developer.
- *Policy analyst.* Policies govern large segments of rural areas, no differently from what one might find in more populated areas. However, rural areas are unique in that, often, resources are

scarcer and communities are more dependent on state and federal entities for support. For example, many rural areas are highly dependent on agriculture and within that industry, the United States Department of Agriculture provides a wide variety of support and services. The rural social worker needs to recognize the importance and value of understanding the impact of agricultural policies. While most think of these as more commercial in nature, a good example is the local and regional impact of organizations such as 4-H and childhood development and programming. Other areas of policy concern are associated with rural economic development, employment, housing, health, mental health, and education.

CURRENT KNOWLEDGE AND PROMISING PRACTICES

Currently, an interest in understanding rural social work is experiencing resurgence. For example, several studies have been conducted focusing on the lack of and need for rural social workers (Ginsberg, 2011; Lohmann & Lohmann, 2005; Mackie, 2008, 2012). In addition, there are attempts to better understand the impact of economic and social changes across rural America (Ulrich, 2010). At this time, what we essentially know about rural social service needs is largely couched in economic terms; rural areas are more likely to struggle with the lack of economic development and the need for sustainable employment, more stable tax bases, and for better and more efficient mental health and social service delivery systems. In rural areas, economics are everything (not unlike, of course, urban areas).

Rural areas differ from urban areas significantly in that, often, there is a lack of economic base due to situations somewhat beyond local control. For example, we know that rural areas lack population, and it is often the human resource pool available that companies consider when deciding to build a factory or develop an economic venture. In fact, this concern was well explored by Carr and Kefalas (2009) when they carefully studied the effects of the "rural brain drain" and found that, too often, youths growing up in rural areas move away after graduating from high school and, as a result, the community loses some of its greatest assets: the human capital. But the youths leave the rural area because they are unable to secure adequate employment or otherwise are drawn away for a myriad of reasons. In the end, these authors are essentially saying that those who leave are typically those who are more talented and have the ability to make valuable social change, and those who remain are unable to obtain the education and skills necessary to advance the community.

We also know that there remains a technological divide between rural and urban areas (Stone, 2011). The author discusses the need for rural areas to be more sophisticated in the access to and use of technology to advance social services as well as grow and develop economically. As we all are well aware, we live in a highly advanced technological society today and, as such, access to technology in any area is critical to future success. In rural areas, this is especially important given that by its own nature, the isolation experienced in these areas can become mitigated through the use of the Internet. According to Stone (2011), the need for high quality access to technology in rural areas crosses all systems levels. For example, the need for health care and social service agencies to be able to record and document casework and make it accessible to other social workers is critical to providing excellent service. Specifically, health care and mental health care services that are otherwise difficult or even impossible to access in isolated areas can be readily accessed when adequate technology is available. Not long ago a patient might lack access to a medical specialist in their area and be forced to travel considerable distance to seek care. Today, opportunities exist that allow the same patient to be "seen" from a distance by a variety of specialists, receive a diagnosis, and ultimately get the appropriate care, thus reducing at least some of the need for travel, the expense, and the process that was associated with receiving the same care in the past.

At the mezzo level, technology serves as a way to connect people to services, programs, and opportunities and "shortens the distance" between people. For example, we know that the rural population is aging. Coupled with what we learned from Carr and Kefalas (2009) we also know that, often, aging parents and grandparents continue to live in rural areas while children and grandchildren live elsewhere in more urbanized places. Properly applied, the use of technology can connect people with care systems and services that bridge resources and create useful, sustainable connections. Specifically, today's technology allows people to remain connected though audio and visual media, and in the event that a problem were to occur, people can immediately communicate a need for services with little more than a push of a button or through a monitoring device.

At the macro level, technology is highly effective in connecting otherwise rural and isolated areas with places more populated. Given the postindustrial nature of the American economy, today more than ever before communities can connect and communicate with each other in new and dynamic ways. For example, cottage industries and those who work in industries that allow the use of technology as a medium for exchange can essentially work from anywhere, be it a coffee shop in St. Louis or a rural homestead in central Alaska. The use of technology in rural areas also allows communities to focus on economic development in ways not otherwise available in the past. Rural areas are often where natural or base resources are extracted and then sent on to more urbanized areas for processing. In today's technological era, those resources can be more efficiently managed through greater connectedness with the "outside" world. For example, Minnesota is a large producer of lumber, iron ore, corn, and soybeans. Rural communities are highly dependent on the extraction of these base resources for economic well-being. In the past, it was more difficult to connect between those who harvest, mine, or otherwise extract these resources with those who later mill, smelt, or process the materials. Today, there is more opportunity than ever to combine these processes and enhance the efficiencies between the two processes.

All of the discussion around the need for high-quality technology in rural areas hinges on whether or not those resources actually exist (Mackie, 2015). For many in rural America, access to technology such as the Internet has arrived and, as a result, shrunk the distance between parties. However, places still remain where access is limited and even nonexistent. In those places where access to technology does exist, too often the financial cost of access to the Internet remains high compared to service prices in more populated areas. For the rural social worker, understanding the importance of the need for access to technology is paramount to practicing well as a generalist, and, when access is limited or lacking, it should be seen as a challenge. The growth and development of rural areas is closely tied to technology. Here is where community action and organization skills are becoming increasingly important for social workers in rural areas.

Another of the many challenges facing rural social services is the lack of providers willing and interested in working in more remote locations. Research on this question by Mackie (2008, 2012) found that there are key predictors of who is more or less likely to become a rural social worker. Specifically, it was found that those who grew up in a rural area, social work students who completed their practicum in a rural location, and those who received rural-specific content during their social work education were more likely to become social workers in rural areas compared to those who did not have these traits. Those who grew up in a rural area are more likely to find rural life favorable, desire living in a familiar area, or choose to live near family and friends. Students who complete practicums in rural areas are believed to be those who may have initially sought out placement in this environment based on their own rural background, coupled with the opportunities to get hired at the agency upon graduation. For those who were exposed to rural-specific content, it is likely that they were essentially acculturated to the ideas of what rural practice entails and were prepared to practice in this unique environment. Interestingly, it is likely that the very things that draw one group to wanting to practice in a rural area repel others. Those who grew up in rural places often share that they prefer the laid-back, more easygoing lifestyle that rural areas provide, whereas those who grew up in more populated areas see this as a detriment and less appealing. Perhaps in the end, those who grew up in rural areas simply calibrate their expectations differently from those who grew up in urban locations. Rural-raised individuals appear more likely to seek out a quiet, slower-paced life and to reside in what is, to them, familiar spaces and environments.

PROMISING PRACTICES: WHAT WORKS IN RURAL AREAS?

Community Organizing: Two Theoretical Models

Community organizing is often considered the stalwart of macro practice in social work. It is here that we can focus on bringing together and improving the quality of life for those who are oppressed, disempowered, or marginalized and do so in such a way as to create sustainable, stakeholder-based actions that, when done correctly, turn over the "power" to the people most invested. But how do we do this? What are the theoretical models that guide our work? While there are many different approaches, nearly all are grounded in two basic models, the conflict model developed by Saul Alinsky (1971) and the consensus model developed by Michael Eichler (2007). Each presents with unique positives and negatives but both are effective when employed properly.

Alinsky's Conflict Model for Community Organizing

Saul David Alinsky was born January 30, 1909, in Chicago, the son of Russian Jewish immigrants. Growing up with a certain amount of anti-Semitism and often poor, Alinsky developed his belief that if you want social or political power, all too often you have to take it from those who have it, because people in positions of power are unlikely to just give it away. From this basic assumption, he went on to develop several clever and logical "rules for radicals" that focused on how to gain community power among people, especially the poor. Working largely in impoverished neighborhoods, Alinsky helped people organize around common goals, fight those who were blocking forward movement, and develop sustainable organizations among the poor. Abbreviated outlines of Alinsky's rules are as follows*:

Rule 1: Power is not only what you have, but what an opponent thinks you have.
Rule 2: Never go outside the experience of your people.

Rule 3: Whenever possible, go outside the experience of the opponent.

Rule 4: Make the opponent live up to their own rules.

Rule 5: Ridicule is your most potent weapon.

Rule 6: A good tactic is one your people enjoy and want to participate in.

Rule 7: A tactic that drags on too long weighs down the group and inertia sets in—avoid it.

Rule 8: Keep the pressure on the opponent.

Rule 9: The threat is usually more frightening to the opposition than the thing itself.

Rule 10: The major premise of tactics is the development of an operation that will maintain a constant pressure on the opposition.

Rule 11: If you push a negative hard and deep enough it will break through to the other side.

Rule 12: The price of a successful attack is a constructive compromise.

Rule 13: Pick the target, freeze it, personalize it, and polarize it.

*Abbreviated rules from Mackie, P.F.E. (2009).

Alinsky's work focused on how to get power, how to use it, and, ultimately, how to keep it among the poor. It has been described as antagonistic, confrontational, and radical. It required a certain amount of aggressive response to social injustices and, thus, is not always well received. Not everyone feels as comfortable as Alinsky did in being so forceful and forward. Others feel that it is better to work with, not against, others. Here is where Eichler (2007) enters into the discussion.

Eichler's Consensus Model for Community Organizing

Michael Eichler was educated as a social worker and considered working in a state of consensus a more appropriate approach to conflict resolution than engaging in Alinsky's conflict-based methods. In this approach, Beck and Eichler (2000) and Eichler (2007) seek to find areas of mutual agreement between otherwise disagreeing parties. The consensus model brings forward a set of theoretical arguments grounded in the position that, unlike assumptions under the conflict model, this model's practitioners believe "power does not have to be redistributed but it can be grown, mutual self-interest provides a powerful tool for change, people often behave in reasonable ways when given reasonable choices, and alliance that support social justice goals can be formed between people of divergent backgrounds" (Beck & Eichler, 2000, p. 87). Ultimately, the consensus model seeks to connect the self-interest of community members to the self-interest of others in pursuit of a common goal bound by the theory of social capital (Eichler, 2007).

Like the conflict model, the consensus model puts forward a body of eight tactics or "rules" to guide the practitioner and the practice. To be successful, the consensus-based organizer needs to recognize that achieving sustainable change requires more than simply bringing divergent groups together to discuss the problem, and then walk away thinking that now that all are at the same table, a reasonable, rational, and satisfactory fix will result. Sadly, we are all aware that even well-meaning and thoughtful people will become locked into a state of disagreement with little hope of compromise or resolution. This said, Eichler proposes the following rules to guide the process:

1. Block out your preferences. There is little use of engaging in consensus organizing if you arrive with a predetermined plan and expect the community to follow it. The author suggests that if you have already developed your own preconceived notions about how to proceed, the best approach is to put it away and ignore it the best that you can. The risk here is that you will exert unnecessary influence on the process with your bias. Allow community stakeholders to develop their own ideas.
2. Don't focus on causes. Too often, people come together to pursue positive change. Immediately, there is the real risk of the group seeking to identify the cause of the problem, which will likely create a hopeless environment of blaming. The consensus organizer understands this and works to steer the group away

from engaging in the "blame game" and, instead, focuses on the expected outcomes.

3. Get specific. Eichler warns that nothing gets done with only general agreement—you need to be specific about goals, tasks, and expectations. Community members must be able to specifically identify what they are expected to accomplish, how they are going to accomplish it, and why.

4. Progress through honesty. To be trusted, the consensus organizer must be a truth broker. In addition, the organizer does not manipulate people; they create opportunities to achieve goals by stakeholders interested in reaching a positive goal.

5. Explore options. The organizer is an "ideas collector" and, as such, all reasonable problem-solving options need to be explored regardless of who presents them.

6. Get commitment. For a strategy to be effective, stakeholders must be committed to the process or activity, and commitment is derived from knowing the specific direction in which to go. For commitment to be real and lasting, the goal must be focused and visible.

7. Take the piano off your back. Remember that the final strategies selected must be from the group, not from you. If the group has engaged in a careful plan and prepared to implement it then that is the plan, even if you disagree. Your job was to lead the group where they wanted to go. It was never your responsibility to exert your influence and create your own plan.

8. EZ credit. Pass out credit in the form of genuine compliments and acknowledgment of individual contributions. Let people know how their participation was crucial to the process publicly and privately.

Each of the stated approaches to organizing (Alinsky's and Eichler's) present with positives and negatives, and the usefulness of each is to be determined by the social work practitioner (Mackie & Leibowitz, 2013). Ultimately the question we must all answer when seeking to organize people is, which approach is most appropriate? The Alinsky model assumes that those with power have little to no real or genuine interest in relinquishing power, and thus power must be stripped from them. On the other hand, Eichler's model assumes that each group has a shared understanding of self-interest among members of each group. In this shared self-interest environment, each group can develop responses that will benefit each and avoid the need for further confrontation. The Eichler model assumes that there is a desire for compromise on both sides of the issue. When this is not the case among those currently holding power, Eichler admits that Alinsky's model may be most appropriate. However, Eichler also argues that with adequate conversation and understanding, there is often little need to escalate to the conflict model—which is when the consensus approach is more appropriate and effective.

Regardless of whether one applies the Alinsky or Eichler model, the central question is, do these approaches work among rural populations? Fortunately, evidence exists in case studies of where these approaches were applied in a rural setting and were found to be effective. Let us begin with conflict-model examples as they were applied in rural areas.

CONFLICT-BASED COMMUNITY ORGANIZING FROM A RURAL PERSPECTIVE: TWO CASE STUDIES

In 1978, Senator Paul Wellstone published *How the Rural Poor Got Power: Narrative of a Grass-Roots Organizer*. This book describes how Wellstone and the organization he founded, the Organization for a Better Rice County (OBRC) in south-central Minnesota, organized the rural poor around Alinsky's (1971) radical community organizing methods and addressed the unique concerns of rural residents from a macro practice standpoint. Wellstone describes the complexities of organizing rural residents, especially those who are poor and disempowered, with the following excerpt:

In rural communities, the political systems and power constraints are different (or modified) for those in urban communities. The rural poor are not heirs of a tradition of political activism and attempted organization, as are many urban communities. Organizing is difficult where there is no expectation for social change and where the assertion of dignity often leads to retaliation. Low-income residents are isolated from one another and from more affluent sectors of the community. They are stigmatized for being poor. Sanctions against rural dissidents can be effectively enforced, for rural, small-town communities lack the more elaborate organizational life and impersonal economy found in urban areas. There are few voluntary organizations to which the poor can appeal. Legal service programs are usually nonexistent. In short, low-income people are extremely vulnerable to economic, social, and physical retaliation. They face many obstacles and restraints in trying to voice their concerns and influence local government. (p. viii)

As you read this excerpt, what questions arise for you? A few questions might be: This statement was based on observations and experiences from the mid-1970s and, as such, do they remain relevant for today? Are the rural poor really so disadvantaged and oppressed as to be described as stigmatized? Is this population really subject to retaliation when they attempt to organize in such a way as to improve their own living conditions?

According to Wellstone and the OBRC at the time, many of the rural poor in Rice County, Minnesota, were subject to poor living conditions, unhealthy housing, and lack of access to public food programs administered by the county board of commissioners. The attempt to organize the poor initially fell short. Landlords intimidated renters, and the county board of commissioners labeled the OBRC members as agitators. In turn, the poor were afraid that if they participated in OBRC activities, they too would be labeled as agitators and experience retaliation from county commissioners, landlords, and other residents. This fear was an effective strategy for those in positions of authority to maintain their power over the poor.

But the poor have rights, right? Are there not laws that protect families and individuals from unsafe housing, hunger, bullying, and intimidation from elected officials? Of course there are—but laws are only as effective as they are enforceable. Wellstone and his colleagues organized several families around tenant rights across the county and secured the services of a local attorney to represent them—pro bono. The attorney assured the families that their arguments were legally sound and he would provide them with adequate support to carry the case forward to the courts if necessary. Unfortunately, none of the families took legal action. According to Wellstone, tenant rights organizing was difficult due to one critical element—an extreme shortage of low-cost housing. Rural renters were painfully aware of their own reality, which was if they did fight for and receive some level of justice around tenant rights they could simultaneously price themselves out of the housing market. In a final analysis, Wellstone and the OBRC found that insufficient work had been done on their part. Renters were largely unfamiliar with "tenant rights," had never heard of the OBRC, and many were convinced by landlords that the OBRC was little more than a group of local college prelaw students who were "trying out their training on you" (p. 10).

Real or not, these were the perceptions of the people the OBRC was trying to help, and the propaganda from the landlords was effective. In the end, the people who did not trust their landlords trusted the OBRC even less. The OBRC was a relatively new organization with no real successes to its credit, nothing to point to so as to show that they were worthy of people's trust. This is a critical observation for us as rural social workers addressing community organizing to investigate further. The OBRC was able to establish credibility among the rural poor of Rice County, Minnesota, by approaching the group differently.

Wellstone and the OBRC recognized that the food assistance program designed to provide for the nutritional needs of the poor was sorely inadequate in scope and delivery. Only 20 percent of the eligible population was participating in the program and among those who did participate, they had to go to a single location and wait for hours before they could receive food assistance. The OBRC recognized that the population served by this program had not been given any voice in the process of delivery or distribution. In essence, the poor were forced to accept whatever service was provided and were expected to not take issue with the process. The OBRC assembled a group of eligible recipients and asked them if they preferred to receive food from the commodities program (where people received actual food) or the Food Stamp program (administered by the

Department of Agriculture where participants could exchange food vouchers for food at participating grocery stores). The OBRC then presented their report on the inefficiencies of the county food program to the local newspaper, which ran a story that outlined the problems with the program. In response, the director of the county welfare department and the chairperson of the county welfare board spoke on the radio denouncing the OBRC—which made the group recognizable and a household name. The credibility of the OBRC was being established. The OBRC called a public meeting among the poor to discuss the costs and benefits of the commodity food and the Food Stamp programs. After much debate, the people decided that they wanted to keep the commodity program, but with better quality foods, another distribution center in the county, and reduce the waiting time for the food. The group received a public hearing in front of the welfare board, and the people presented their concerns. The result was the creation of another distribution center, an increase in staff to administer the program, more vegetables and meat, chairs for people to sit while they waited, and the creation of an outreach program to educate eligible people about the food program. This was the success the OBRC needed to establish them as a credible organization and to develop true grassroots support from those directly affected.

This community organizing action was effective in many ways. It recognized the need for rural residents to have a voice while, at the same time, the political reality they lived in. The county board was not initially interested in expanding the food program in any real way, but with sufficient political pressure, they did so. This action also did what a good action must do—include those most in need of the reform, which in this case were the rural poor of Rice County.

Another example of rural community organizing in a small community environment is described by Mackie (2009). The author started a grassroots community organizing activity around the need to protect a neighborhood against property developers also using Saul Alinsky's organizing tactics (Alinsky, 1971). Mackie and local residents grew frustrated over time with property developers who were buying up older homes in an otherwise affordable area and converting them into high-density rental properties. The problem was that as home prices and values were increasing, lower and middle income individuals and families were finding it more difficult to buy a home and, thus, were often limited to renting. Land developers were drawn to properties in this neighborhood for the same reasons as the potential buyers—affordability. The problem was not a lack of rental properties in the community, but a lack of affordable houses.

In response, a group of neighbors organized and began working to rezone the neighborhood. Rezoning was seen as the most efficient and effective way to reduce the conversion of single family homes into rental properties in that, at the time the group formed, a developer could put up to five unrelated people per unit together. This resulted in up to ten or more (mostly) adults living in a structure originally designed for a much lower density. While increasing the total number of people living in a house was economically beneficial to landlords, it created challenges in the neighborhood for other residents. To make matters worse, there was considerable conflict between rental property owners and single family home owners. Rental properties were not often maintained well and were all too often the source of noise, garbage, and upkeep violations. Rezoning to only having a maximum of two unrelated people living in a unit significantly reduced the profitability of the rental, and worked as a disincentive to convert a home into a lease property. It also served to stabilize the neighborhood and encourage homes to be purchased by single families. This activity was successful and worked; the neighborhood was rezoned, stabilized, and the affordability of single family homes was maintained.

Like Wellstone, Mackie found that rural residents do not have the same level of social justice expectations as one might find in more urbanized locations. Many local residents liked the idea of rezoning and stabilizing the neighborhood but were afraid of retaliation from landlords or an apathetic response from the city government. There had been an attempt to rezone about twenty years prior, with no real interest or support from the political powers at the time. Some residents were harassed by landlords and "encouraged" to stop participating in the rezoning efforts, whereas others had sunk into a state of inertia and were simply not interested in getting involved. Some residents shared that this was a close-knit community "where people know people" and long-term enemies could be created easily. The local sociocultural reality directly influenced individual and group behavior. People were not used to seeing successful grassroots action, were worried about how they would be perceived in the community, and were not entirely sure of how to organize in any real and productive way.

Mackie brought together interested individuals with shared concerns. Petitions were collected, and the planning and zoning commission was asked to hear the case. This small but significant success was seen as positive momentum by many in the neighborhood, and as a threat by the land developers. The night of the public planning and zoning commission meeting is best described as spirited and raucous. Both sides arrived with their people, though the neighborhood residents had clearly been assembled and prepared more systematically than the landlord opposition group. The commission opened the floor for discussion about rezoning, and both sides took turns discussing their concerns. After about one hour of testimony, one final resident went to the podium and stated that he was sick and tired of absentee landlords taking their rent but leaving their problems. After some deliberation, the commission voted unanimously to support the rezoning request. Six weeks later, the city council agreed and a neighborhood consisting of approximately six hundred homes was rezoned. The people had won.

All organizers know that winning a battle such as this in a small community is extremely important. Too often, residents who live in "fishbowl" environments know that given the close nature of relationships in communities such as these, people can get sidetracked from the issue at hand. Instead of discussing the problem, it is easy to digress and focus on all of the wrong elements—specific people, past events or activities, behaviors. What is especially important to remember always in organizing people in small communities is that remaining focused on the target is not only essential, it is paramount to the success of the activity. Not unlike Wellstone's (1978) discussion on developing people-power in a rural community, Mackie (2009) was able to tap into a power relationship residents already held in the community—but didn't know it at the beginning. An assembled people focused on making social or political change can do so even if they lack financial resources. As a group, they can exert power from the mass of energy created when one brings together interested stakeholders to work on a common goal. Wellstone and Mackie each assembled people using Alinsky's methods designed to bring people together to address a commonly held problem.

CONSENSUS-BASED COMMUNITY ORGANIZING FROM A RURAL PERSPECTIVE: A CASE STUDY

As stated earlier, there are two general approaches to organizing people, the conflict model and the consensus model. Each has unique qualities, and each can be effective. The conflict model developed by Saul Alinsky has been in use much longer, and, therefore, there are more case examples available to show its effectiveness. In contrast, the conflict model as developed by Mike Eichler and detailed in the book *Consensus Organizing: Building Communities of Mutual Self-Interest* (2007) is a much newer development. Therefore, there are fewer actual case studies available to use as examples. However, a review of several recent community organizing activities in rural areas shows that the consensus model, either by plan or by default, has become infused into the process. This seems only natural in that the unique social and cultural dynamics of rural areas fit well with a more consensus-minded approach to social development. This case study describes an example of a successful consensus-focused community organizing project aimed at increasing access to dental services by low-income children and their families in rural northern Minnesota (Larson, 2009).

Northern Minnesota contains a vast area of rural wilderness and remote communities. One of the many challenges experienced in this region is access to affordable dental care, especially among low-income children and families. In 2003, a concerned group of people identified this as a real and pervasive concern in the Beltrami County area. Several key health care providers and related constituents agreed that there was indeed a problem associated with access to dental care among this group, but they were challenged to determine appropriate strategies to address the need. The stakeholders concluded that to be effective in developing a planned response that would be effective, they needed to develop a coalition of appropriate stakeholders who could develop this resource. Grounded in Winer and Ray's (1994) process of building community collaboration, they engaged in this consensus-type process. This included developing an understanding of the history of collaboration and becoming educated about what linkages have already been established. Approaching the process with mutual respect for all parties and developing trust between stakeholders was identified as paramount to the process. Next, they focused on identifying and recruiting an appropriate cross-section of group members. This encourages greater participation and buy-in on the part of the community. They then focused on assisting members of the coalition to see the collaboration as in their own best self-interest. Larson (2009) argues that when participants focus on their self-interests, it serves as an offset from the concerns associated with the loss of autonomy individuals may otherwise experience. Next, there was an acknowledgment that there is a need to give participants permission to engage in compromise. Representatives needed a certain amount of latitude to make decisions and work out agreements to keep the project moving forward. Once these baselines were set in place, it was recognized that there is a need for allowing multiple layers of decision making, which allows for different concerns to be addressed instead of attempting to solve all problems at once or in one particular way. Open and frequent communication was encouraged, concrete and attainable goals and objectives were identified, a shared vision was developed, a skilled convener employed to address sticking points and keep the process moving, and sufficient funds allocated.

Through the application of Winer and Ray's (1994) community collaboration model, the coalition was able to eventually develop, implement, and support a rural dental facility that focused on specific and agreed upon objectives such as pain and disease reduction and increased preventive care and even specialty care among this population. A review of Eichler's (2007) model shows considerable similarity. According to Larson (2009), some of the most important elements to this type of project are to focus on collaboration, community buy-in, and maintaining respect among stakeholders. When these critical elements are in place, positive outcomes can come as a result. Eichler (2007) focuses on the same elements, stating that there are ways in which stakeholders can identify their own self-interests, which will encourage further buy-in.

Over time, more case studies will likely be developed around the practice of consensus organizing, and in fact some organizations are now employing these techniques. For example, the organization Neighborworks America has encouraged the development of case studies from rural areas where consensus organizing has been used to enhance human rights and opportunities. One of these examples was presented at the Neighborworks America New Rural America Symposium in 2005 (Neighborworks America, 2011). The Quitman County Development Organization (QCDO) in the delta region of Mississippi was created in 1977 to address challenges around the lack of support and recognition of the largely African American population by community institutions. Founders of the QCDO had concluded that African Americans and their social concerns were not represented on the city, county, or state levels. It was argued that educational and financial institutions were not serving the African American community in the same way that they were among members of the dominant culture—deeply embedded and institutional racism was keeping an entire group of people from being able to fully participate in society. A group of QCDO leaders first facilitated a peaceful nine-day protest and organized a boycott of purchasing goods from local stores. While this appears at first to be more of the conflict organizing approach, it created the stress necessary to encourage community members to come together and begin talks about what the African American community needed and was not receiving. Members of the local African American community began to run for elected offices, participate in planning projects, and work with other community members to resolve differences and rectify past discrimination. In 1987, Quitman County, Mississippi, elected the largest number of African Americans at one time to public office ever seen in the United States. Over time, the QCDO continued to develop community-focused entities such as the First Delta Federal Credit Union in 1981, the Youth Opportunities Unlimited Daycare Center in 1994, The Big River Housing Development Corporation in 1989, and the Microenterprise and Business Development Program in 1998. Through the use of consensus organizing, underrepresented groups of people in this county were able to not only gain the recognition they richly deserved, but to apply that energy into the development of a financial institution, housing, youth services, education, and a business program.

One can see that organizing people in rural areas is at the center of accomplishing the goals and objectives of the residents. At this time there are two basic approaches to organizing: the conflict model and the consensus model. It is impossible to state which is better, because each contain positives and negatives. The goal of the rural social worker engaged in this type of work is to apply the most appropriate model and do so in such a way as to gain the greatest benefit. There is no specific formula for determining which approach is most appropriate, but there are some suggestions. First, one must determine how much social power the oppressed group has at their disposal. Specifically, are there enough people to effectively organize? Can those currently in the power positions see the benefit of self-interest in working with another group to resolve conflict? Is there buy-in that the problem is one that may have viable and workable solutions, or do those in power positions disagree that a problem even exists? How much human capital does a group have to carry out a long (and potentially exhausting) series of conflict protests and related activities? Finally, one must ultimately ask, how comfortable is a group with engaging in one approach over the other? If an advocate does not have buy-in and an investment among those seeking change, it is highly unlikely that much of any real change will ever occur.

RURAL ECONOMIC DEVELOPMENT

Encouraging economic development is hardly unique in either rural or urban environments. Read any newspaper, surf the Internet, listen to news radio, or watch the television on any given day across the United States and you will likely find a discussion about the need for economic development, creation of jobs, or stabilization of a local economy. While there are similarities between rural and urban challenges, rural areas face unique challenges not otherwise typical in a more urbanized place. Too often, the lack of employment in rural areas is grounded in three main problem areas: (1) Local economies dependent on a small number of employers (lack of economic diversity), (2) geographic isolation, and (3) lack of natural and human capital and resources. Each of these challenges mentioned presents with a multitude of complicating factors within themselves.

Rural areas are often highly dependent on a small number of primary employers, which creates a serious problem if one or more of those employers fails. For example, in the prairie states a local economy is often deeply grounded in agriculture. When commodity prices are high and there is an increased demand for farm products, employment opportunities increase. However, when commodity prices are low and the demand for agricultural industry labor is low, unemployment increases and opportunities for employment shrink. This dependence on jobs directly related to a natural resource is common across rural areas, whether it be in the farm, forest, mining, or fishing industries.

In rural areas that are not as dependent on natural resources, there is often dependence on other single economics such as tourism or manufacturing. For example, rural areas of southern and central Michigan are often dependent on the manufacturing of material used by the automobile industry—suppliers to the large automobile companies in and around Detroit. These are typically smaller companies who manufacture products under contract for Ford, Chrysler, and General Motors Corporations. In these areas, the smaller, rural-based companies produce goods that are then shipped to the assembly lines in the more metropolitan areas. When the demand for automobiles is high, the demand for these parts is predictably high as well. When demand for automobiles falters, so goes the demand for the parts manufactured in these rural areas—areas that are more disproportionately dependent on these single manufacturers compared to what is typically found in urban areas. In short, when the main employer in a small town stops producing, there are fewer employment alternatives for those out of work.

Compounding the problem further, in rural and small communities there is a greater dependence on tax and income revenue generated by the main employers. In these areas, when a major employer slows production or closes, the resources that supported other local businesses suffer as well. For example, imagine that a small manufacturing company in a rural area that employs a significant number of the local population closes. The workers are now unemployed and, as a result, will spend less in the other local businesses. Worse, if these workers are unable to find new employment locally they will likely have to move away, and, without jobs, new people will likely not move into the community. The overall generation of taxes and capital resources is reduced, leaving the community challenged to meet the needs of those who remain. The spiral downward can have devastating effects on a rural community. The overall lack of economic diversity in many of the United States rural areas is a constant and chronic problem.

The geographic isolation associated with rural areas can negate the opportunity of economic growth and development. Rural areas are by nature isolated, and, thus, it is challenging to attract diverse employers due to transportation costs, the lack of capital, and the lack of human resources. Imagine owning a company that manufactures fishing equipment. While on the surface it may make sense to seek a place to manufacture your products near a beautiful remote lake or river in the mountains of Colorado, you would instead be more interested in a location's proximity to major highways to transport in raw material and send out finished products. You would also be interested in locating your business in an area that has an ample population of people to work in your factory. Without either of these resources, you would be challenged to produce these goods, regardless of how aesthetically pleasing the area may be. In the same vein, if you own a river rafting company, you are less dependent on road access and more dependent on the existence of a river that can be navigated, but you remain highly dependent on people's ability to get to your location.

While the issue of human capital has already been touched on, this is an area of utmost importance in rural economic development. Human capital is one of the most important natural resources available for employment creation and local economic development. In the book *Hollowing Out the Middle: The Rural Brain Drain and What It Means for America* by Carr and Kefalas (2009), the lack of human resources in rural areas is identified as one of the singular most important problems in rural areas today. The authors discuss the problems associated with the exodus of youths from rural areas and the impact this is having upon rural areas. They identify four main groups of youths from rural areas: (1) the Achievers, (2) the Stayers, (3) the Seekers, and (4) the Returners.

The Achievers are those who cannot find reason enough to remain in a rural area due to the lack of opportunities available. These are the rural youths who leave for college and remain gone after graduation. They are often those whom a rural community has placed a great amount of resources into—education, extracurricular activities, sports, and overall encouragement. These are the high-achieving students expected to someday leave with an understanding that they will likely not come back. At the same time, they are also those who are more likely to go out into the world and become successful leaders in other, often more metropolitan, communities—exactly what rural areas need. In a sense, this is human capital that the community desperately needs but, at the same time, expects to leave.

The Stayers are those who do not see themselves as people who would or even can leave where they grew up. According to the authors, this group is largely comprised of local youths who may not have excelled in school, did not show promise for growth and development, or who would likely not continue on with further education at any distance from where they grew up. When post–high school education is pursued, it is likely to be in the form of technical or trades training and not university-level education. These are the people who will likely not venture very far from their hometowns for any extended period of time. This group represents who is likely going to mature into the future leaders of the community, the workers at the local businesses, the future of rural America. The authors argue that these are not people incapable of being successful in higher education or leadership, but that they are simply unprepared for such direction. In fact, the authors express concern that not enough is being done for this group of rural residents given the importance of their place on the socioeconomic ladder of their communities. These are the people who grow to serve as members of local school boards, township trustees, county board members, zoning commissioners, city council members, volunteer fire fighters, and members of civic organizations. In a sense, the Stayers are the very people who are the next generation of the rural populous and the very group who will influence the future of rural America. Or at a minimum they will be the receivers of what comes of rural areas.

The authors identify the Seekers as those from small towns and rural areas who for whatever reason have a sense of adventure, but too often bear little in the way of advanced human capital. They are the ones who do the implausible such as join the Navy even though they are from the Sand Hills of Nebraska and have never seen the ocean except for the images on the television or perhaps while on a family vacation. This is the adventurous group who typically follow the military path as a "way out." Additionally, Seekers are often those who have the desire to attend college or advanced training in the future but may not have the resources to do so. Today's military offers considerable educational and other benefits that are attractive to Seekers. This is the group who possesses a certain human capital that can be beneficial to the community, but feel they must leave the community to procure external resources necessary to expand their options. The military is a natural fit for the Seekers in that it provides the option of leaving, a job, excitement, and future growth opportunities.

The final group identified by Carr and Kefalas (2009) are the Returners. Returners are those who left (either as Achievers or Seekers) and later returned. Within this group is the subgroup, the Boomerangs. Boomerangers are largely Seekers who left for a short period of time (say for a military enlistment or after a few years in college) and then return to their home community and become reabsorbed into the Stayer group without much attention or fanfare. Boomerangers live "between the groups" in that they have acquired additional skills, experiences, and knowledge that is advanced compared to the Stayers but less than what is found among the Achievers. It can be difficult for Boomerangers to fully integrate back into the community due to these advanced intercommunity experiences. Interestingly, Boomerangers tend to be female whereas Stayers are more likely to be male. As a result, females often have more education and life experience outside of the community, which can result in a certain level of conflict and competition between the genders. A smaller but important subgroup among the Returners group are the High-Flyers. This group is comprised of Achievers who return with high levels of education, life experience, and knowledge with the expectation that they can reattach to their rural community roots. They have made the conscious choice to live in a rural location for a multitude of reasons, but most are grounded in the pursuit of meeting personal lifestyle choice needs as well as in working to assist their communities and help address the problems of the community. This is the smallest group identified by the authors. Over all, Achievers tend to leave and never return, which is reminiscent of an old axiom still heard in rural communities, "The county line must be the edge of the earth because when people cross it, they never come back."

While there is significant room for debate about the different groups described above and how they are portrayed, Carr and Kefalas have at a minimum identified differences between groups and how the social structure may be comprised in rural areas. Perhaps, more importantly, they have also identified critical human resource elements in rural communities. Specifically, we are aware of the historic out-migration of rural populations to more urbanized areas and the negative effects this has on rural communities (Cashwell & Just, 2008). What is important to social workers practicing in rural areas is to understand the cascading effects of this out-migration and the impact losing the Achievers has on these communities. The very skills and abilities such as higher education, leadership, and technical skills needed to build, rebuild, maintain, and improve a rural community leave each spring with the conclusion of high school commencement ceremonies. In fact, according to Carr and Kefalas's (2009) findings, community members have come to expect this to occur and even encourage it. They understand that opportunities for their youths may not exist in rural America and that for these youths to maximize their potential, they must leave. In essence, rural America is rearing youths who will go elsewhere and increase the human capital of another community, often with the blessing of the community who otherwise raised, educated, and invested in them. The very people rural communities need to retain are also the same who are least likely to stay. This has damaging social implications. How must it feel to be told that as a Stayer you are not the "cream of the crop"? You are a member of a group who does not have the human capital resources to advance your community and one who is more likely to struggle to meet your own needs, to pay your bills, to have a quality life. Is this what being a Stayer means? Part of what a social worker is expected to do in a rural area is to not support or participate in getting caught up in this type of denigrating mind-set. The Stayers are the members of the community you work with, call friends, and otherwise live with as a community. A social worker will instead seek ways of enhancing human capital and improving the quality of life within the community instead of participating in a process that essentially creates more barriers and more challenges. In social work we often state that "we start with where the client is." Here, the client is multifaceted in that the client is both the individual and the community, as well as the individual in the community. The collective consciousness of a group of people who are dependent upon each other in one form or another is the "community." Dig into a rural community and one finds that rural residents have the same wants and needs of more urban counterparts. For example, rural residents want economic growth and development, good schools, low crime rates, low unemployment, low poverty levels, and clean and safe communities. Among those currently living in these communities, they also want to stay. Rarely if ever will one find someone living in a rural community encouraging high unemployment and marginal schools. Too much energy is focused on the Achievers and the High-Flyers, and not enough on the Stayers. The third group is the dominant group of people who live and work in rural America. Therefore, it is imminently important to focus on their needs and identify their strengths if we are to strengthen rural communities. There is a need to refocus energies toward finding new and dynamic yet concrete ways to assist rural communities. One way this can be accomplished is by developing a deep understanding of what resources are available.

RESOURCES FOR RURAL ECONOMIC DEVELOPMENT

When discussing the challenges of economic development in rural areas, it is important to understand that the problem is not only about physical or tangible resources, but about human resources. Too often when young people leave rural areas, they do not return. This leads to a lack of human capital stock by which to build future capital, human or otherwise. One of the many components of the position of the rural social worker is to find ways in which to encourage those who leave to return, and those who stay to expand their knowledge, skills, and abilities in ways that benefit the overall quality of the community. This can be a daunting task, but social workers in rural areas do not simply "provide therapy" or serve as caseworkers. It is more complex. The social worker in a rural area needs to be generalist in nature. There is a need to understand the complexities of the interconnectedness of a variety of systems, to serve as a bridge between groups, and to be able to advocate for and even acquire needed resources to benefit the community.

Identifying and acquiring resources in rural communities can be difficult. For example, imagine a social worker in an area with low home ownership levels within the community. It is known that home ownership is one of the best ways for people to acquire wealth over time (the wealth is in the property value that should increase over time). Home ownership in rural areas is higher than what is found in metropolitan areas; 76 percent of rural residents own their own home compared to 70 percent in metropolitan areas. At the same time, rural families are three times more likely to reside in mobile homes compared to their more urban counterparts (Cashwell & Just, 2008), and mobile homes are less valuable and depreciate in value at a much faster rate than foundation-built homes. To complicate the housing situation further, approximately 15 percent of rural counties are identified as housing stressed, meaning rural housing is often too costly relative to a family's income, too crowded, or lacking basic facilities within the domain (Cashwell & Just, 2008). At the same time, rural median annual incomes are typically lower than what is found in metropolitan areas. For example, rural median incomes tend to be about 30 percent lower than what is found in urban incomes, and about 14 percent of rural households are considered poor, compared to about 12 percent of urban households (Cashwell & Just, 2008). These numbers become starker in that according to Miller and Weber (2004), 95 percent of all counties with a poverty rate of over 20 percent are identified as rural, and rural child poverty rates are consistently higher across all areas of the United States when compared to urban areas (Cashwell and Just, 2008). Given the information provided here, it is apparent that salaries are typically lower in rural areas and residents may find it difficult to save enough money for the initial down payment or meet a lender's income expectations for a home loan, and, as a result, it's likely they may not be able to eventually buy their own home. What options does a rural social worker have to address this problem?

Often, state and federal government agencies support programs designed to support rural social and economic development. For example, the United States Department of Agriculture (USDA) Office of Rural Development (2011) maintains offices and contacts in each of the fifty states, and provides grants and loans to assist rural residents to repair, restore, improve, and even purchase homes. Specifically, this agency offers resources to purchase or maintain a home in a rural area for people with low incomes in the forms of guaranteed loans, direct loans, and other approaches. These programs are means tested, meaning they are based on the means in which an individual or family is able to pay back the loan. For example, applicants for a federally guaranteed housing loan may have an income up to 115 percent of the median income of the area in which the home is located. The home can be purchased with no down payment, and the lending institution who provides the loan receives a guarantee of repayment by the federal government in the event that the borrower defaults on the loan.

For individuals and families who have even lower incomes, the USDA Rural Development Housing and Community Facilities Loan Assistance program allows for direct loans from the program, which would not include an intermediary bank to provide the loan and then receive a repayment guarantee from the USDA. This direct loan program focuses on two definitions of who can receive this benefit: the "poor" and the "very poor." The very poor are defined as having incomes below 50 percent of the regional area median income (AMI) and the poor are with incomes of 50–80 percent of the AMI. People with what is defined as a "moderate income" (income of 80–100 percent of the AMI) do not qualify for this program and would be directed to the housing loan guarantee program.

Whereas the loan guarantee program allows for the term of a mortgage to be for up to thirty years, the direct loan program extends the mortgage term for up to thirty-three years or for thirty-eight years for those who have incomes below 60 percent of the AMI and cannot afford the monthly payments at the thirty-three-year level. This program allows the opportunity for low-income rural residents who otherwise would not have the opportunity to do so through more traditional home loan processes to pursue the purchase of a home. The importance of a social worker knowing and understanding these programs cannot be understated. The goal of social work is to find ways in which human life can be enhanced, valued, and elevated. Home ownership is one of the many ways where individuals can develop stability and enhance personal wealth and programs such as this can serve to stabilize and support communities.

Closely related to direct and guaranteed home loan products for rural communities, the USDA Office of Rural Development also provides support for other living and dwelling systems as well. For example, Rural Repair and Rehabilitation Grants provide low- and very-low-income rural residents grant opportunities to improve, repair, or modernize dwellings and to remove dangerous or safety hazards. Rural Housing Site Loans provide for the purchase and development of home sites for low- and moderate-income families. Guaranteed Rental Housing Loans provide resources for construction contractors to build homes in areas that lack affordable housing for low- to moderate-income families. Community Facilities Direct and Guaranteed Loans allow for small- and midsized (up to twenty thousand residents) communities to borrow money to build or improve facilities for health care, public safety, and public services. A community must meet a variety of eligibility criteria to qualify for these resources.

In addition to these loan and grant opportunities, there are other options that support the development of economic growth in rural areas. For example, the Rural Business Enterprise Grant (RBEG) program supports economic growth and development in rural areas. Specifically, this program provides between ten thousand and five hundred thousand dollars for land acquisition, renovation of buildings, improvements of infrastructure, pollution control and abatements, training and technical assistance, and jobs training. The focus on this program is to develop small businesses that will create fifty or fewer new employees and have less than one million dollars in projected annual gross revenues.

There are many other programs designed to support and assist rural and small communities, too many to mention further here. This is one of the many challenges facing a rural social worker from a macro perspective. Too often there are resources designed to assist community level concerns, but unfortunately the community members do not always know how to find or where to access these resources. One very good place to begin is at the state level office of the USDA Rural Development office. The USDA maintains state offices of rural development, as well as regional service centers within each state. The regional service centers focus on more regionally appropriate resources, and staff understands local and regional concerns. A regional office locator is available through the USDA Rural Development home page (http://www.rd.usda.gov).

Community Action Agencies (CAAs) are also excellent places for accessing a variety of services in rural communities. CAAs are typically nonprofit organizations (though some may be privately operated) that were founded from the Economic Opportunity Act of 1964 (PL 88-492), legislation led by President Lyndon Johnson in his "War on Poverty." This legislation created and supported a variety of responses to poverty across the United States and was greatly influenced by the dire living conditions witnessed by President Johnson as well as President Kennedy in rural Appalachia and the Deep South (Orleck & Hazirjian, 2011). The purpose of this legislation was to create and maintain a system of services to address a multitude of challenges associated with poverty, with services being provided at the local and community level rather than from a large federal bureaucracy. Community Action Agencies are operated by an executive director and board of directors, which is comprised of members of the community, including members of disadvantaged and underrepresented groups along with local leaders, elected officials, and other individuals from the region the CAA provides services within (Nemon, 2007).

The funding core for CAA programs comes from the Community Services Block Grant (CSBG), which is appropriated by the US Congress under the authority of the Omnibus Reconciliation Act of 1981 (PL 97-35), and was amended in 1998 under Public Law 105-285. While some community action funding comes from the federal budget to provide needed services, most states provide significant funding as well to respond to regional needs. Funding may include money from other grants or financial sources as well. In addition to grants and state and federal aid, CAAs are strongly encouraged to develop programs that generate revenue, which is often done through food programs, thrift store sales, and a variety of services. Programs that often operate under CAAs are the well-known Head Start early education program, heating and utility assistance, home winterization programs, food and nutrition, and services for elderly community members. In short, CAAs focus on providing assistance and services to those considered vulnerable or in need of help at the community level.

PRACTICE APPLICATION

From Paul Olson, MSW

I am a macro practice social worker in the Upper Peninsula (UP) of Michigan. Here, rural takes on new meaning. Everywhere one goes is rural on our peninsula—a landmass roughly equivalent to that of Connecticut, Delaware, New Jersey, and Rhode Island combined, but with a total population of only about three hundred thousand people. Interestingly, if the UP were its own state it would be the only one in the union without even one urban county. The catchment area that my agency is charged with serving includes approximately sixteen thousand square miles—or roughly one-third of the state with a population of about eighteen people per square mile. This can be a remote and isolated place to practice social work.

The services we provide are technical assistance, support, training, and information for schools, governmental bodies, and nonprofit agencies in the region. We are one of the few organizations that provides this kind of assistance across the region. Typically, when organizations are in need of technical support or training, they have to seek services in more populous areas, which are always outside of the UP. The advantage of using our organization over similar outside entities is that these services can be provided in situ, meaning members of this organization are grounded in the local region and have indigenous knowledge and understanding of the region. This provides us with unique opportunities to take into account a client's organizational environment from a truly systems perspective when crafting solutions and responses to their needs.

Among the many limitations we face that are uniquely rural is when working with organizations located in distance places, even though we are otherwise considered "locally located." For example, the main offices of many social service agencies are often located in more populous communities within the region but serve individual clients one hundred or more miles away. This is a significant challenge to service delivery because people going into the field to provide the services may have to drive two hours or more one way to reach even one client. In fact, when agencies contact us for help addressing issues they face with their clients, transportation is often the most noted concern that emerges again and again. Many times, the clients themselves live in geographically isolated locations and if they are also living in poverty (which is often the case and one of the reasons we are now involved), they have trouble accessing transportation for basic necessities such as groceries, education, and health care. When someone is living in such a precarious and fragile financial situation such as this, even the idea of accessing services from community agencies can be considered a luxury.

My organization assists a wide variety of agencies and programs in the use of statistics, data, and information to make programmatic decisions or to pursue funding opportunities. But being in a sparsely populated area has challenges related to data and evidence-based practices, which can lead to something a local judge once called "the tyranny of small numbers." To illustrate, the Michigan child death rate is twenty-seven per one hundred thousand. If a county with a youth population of two thousand had one child under the age of nineteen die, then their "child death rate" would be fifty per one hundred thousand of the population. If, during the next year, there was a car accident where three youths died—the child death rate would skyrocket to one hundred fifty per one hundred thousand. This makes using data very tricky in the sparsely populated counties. Being a macro practice social worker in a region such as this requires me to be constantly aware of situations such as this and interpret the world I live in carefully and thoughtfully.

Another example of challenges associated with being a rural-based macro-practice social worker can be described in the following case from my practice. I was working on a project that was aimed at improving collaboration among organizations that worked with clients in a particular community. As I began to identify the individuals who oversaw services and who actually provided these services, I quickly realized that with the exception of the juvenile court workers, school staff, and the tribal body (this community also has a reservation), most people who worked directly with clients in this area were typically located in a larger town fifty miles away. To call these people together for meetings required considerable negotiation and significant effort on my part. Once this was accomplished, I then had to create experiences sufficiently productive to "make the case" those front-line workers would benefit from these contacts and convince supervisors to support their employees' participation in these meetings and planning activities.

Challenges to practicing rural social work are not limited to only client needs, they include professional needs of other social workers as well. In addition to assisting agencies generally, I also work with a group that focuses on creating adequate continuing education experiences for licensed social workers in this region.

When the state law mandating continuing education for social workers went into effect in 2005, it did not provide for necessary mechanisms to make continuing education hours available to those who live in rural, remote, and otherwise isolated areas such as is commonly found in the UP. While professional firms that specialize in providing continuing education training offered to provide necessary training to social workers in the UP, they did so at a cost, and locally we were at the mercy of the market forces, which many social workers could not afford and agencies could not reimburse for. Especially challenging is our remoteness. The area of the state I cover is too sparsely populated to be attractive to most organizations that could easily provide continuing education. This leaves social workers in my area few choices for completing these mandatory trainings except to travel hundreds of miles. Therefore, I worked to advocate for greater inclusion of training opportunities in the Upper Peninsula to better support the needs of our profession. When you work this remotely, you learn quickly that you are much more dependent on others to be a successful and effective social worker.

COMMON PRACTICE CHALLENGES AND RESPONSES

Common practice challenges associated with macro practice in rural areas focus on access to services, economic development, and the reality that, in rural areas, one is for the most part simply at a distance from resources. Access to services is a chronic problem where attempts have been made to try and better understand the complexities of why rural areas have struggled with recruiting and retaining social workers (Mackie, 2011). In response, social work programs and schools are recognizing the importance of preparing social workers for rural practice and have developed curricula to accomplish this goal. In addition, federal and state governments have developed programs that encourage health care, mental health care, and social service providers to work in rural, isolated, and underdeveloped areas through programs such as the National Health Service Corp (NHSC, 2015). Programs such as this offer salaries, loan repayment, and other assistance to encourage professionals to practice in exchange for specified amounts of time in service. While programs such as these enjoy a certain amount of success, the problem of continuity of care emerges when a care provider works for certain amounts of time, and then vacates the position for more populated areas, leaving the need to recruit a new practitioner.

CONCLUSION

Macro social work practice encompasses many things, crosses the boundaries of all system levels, and focuses on elements that are often difficult to identify and even harder to define. Directly, this area of practice includes actively addressing large social problems that impact and influence rural communities and the people who reside within them. But indirectly, because rural systems are so intertwined, social workers in rural areas will, by either accident or design, find themselves involved in the process of macro work be it through the connection between jobs training and economic development, health care and the need for a clinic, or academic performance and underfunded school districts. Historically, rural social work was largely macro practice. Early in the development of social systems across rural America, it was recognized that there was a need to address transportation issues, communications, education, health care, and government structure. Each of these examples represents macro practice arenas, and, at some point, none existed as we know them today in places where people were settling.

Today, rural areas are experiencing a reverse trend away from the growth observed during the nineteenth and twentieth centuries. In the twenty-first century, we find a rural America losing population and lacking resources. We find higher rates of poverty than before, traditional family farms as we once knew them growing larger and more corporate, and populations of communities thinning. In fact, the term "rural brain drain" has been coined to describe how so many rural youths have left to attend college or seek employment, never to return to their hometowns. Try to imagine the pain, confusion, and even anger that could be attached to such a term among those who choose to remain in more rural locations. It (at least implicitly) implies that if a "brain drain" has occurred among those who left, any term used to describe those who remained would not be flattering. In addition, those who have remained have also watched busy downtowns turn into empty buildings, have experienced falls in property values, and have essentially observed the slow but steady death of their communities. However, not all is so dreary. Understanding the complexities of rural macro practice process allows social workers to be part of the rebuilding process. Here is where individuals can make a significant contribution to restrengthening communities by being able to recognize strengths and assets that may have been overlooked or underutilized previously. It is important to remember that as a strengths-based profession, social work has the capacity to make positive change in the face of hardship.

Related Websites and Other Resources (for Further Learning Opportunities, Discussion Questions):

- National Association for Rural Mental Health at www.narmh.org. The National Association for Rural Mental Health has a long and rich history of advocating for mental health and social services in rural areas, specifically in the area of state and federal policy development. This organization's journal can be accessed at http://www.apa.org/pubs/journals/rmh/index.aspx.
- National Association for Rural Health at www.ruralhealthweb. org. This site is operated by the National Association for Rural Health, which includes professionals focused on rural health and mental health care. This is a very active organization focusing in policy development, legislative advocacy, and education. This organization's journal can be accessed at http://onlinelibrary. wiley.com/journal/10.1111/%28ISSN%291748-0361.
- National Rural Social Work Caucus at www.ruralsocialwork.org. The National Rural Social Work Caucus has long been an ally and advocate for the support and preservation of rural communities and rural social work practice. This organization's journal can be accessed at http://journal.und.edu/crsw/.

- The Rural Sociological Society at www.ruralsociology.org. The
  Rural Sociological Society has been highly engaged in supporting
  research into the complexities of challenges, joys, and actions of
  rural life. This organization's journal can be accessed at
  http://onlinelibrary.wiley.com/journal/10.1111/%28ISSN%291549
  -0831.
- United States Department of Agriculture at www.usda.gov.
  The US Department of Agriculture is much more than a federal
  agency that supports farmers. This agency provides support and
  assistance across rural America by supporting rural economic
  development, housing, food and nutrition programs, youth and
  adult learning, and education in addition to its agricultural
  mission.

5

Beyond the Basics:
Other Issues Facing Social Workers in Rural Places

INTRODUCTION

While much has been written thus far about practicing social work in rural areas from a systems theory perspective, many of the "realities" of rural practice remain to be addressed. This chapter focuses on questions pertaining to culture, politics, and social systems embedded in rural communities. Understanding these realities is to understand deeper meanings within rural communities, and identifying areas of strength and persistence within them. By being able to do this, rural social workers can begin to shape the future in ways that are more lasting and permanent.

RURAL CULTURAL AND SOCIOPOLITICAL REALITIES

At this point of the discussion, it is important to address a cultural and sociopolitical concern that exists in rural areas more so than what is typically found in urbanized areas: social and political conservatism. Considerable evidence suggests that, by and large, rural areas are much more likely to espouse more conservative beliefs and attitudes among the general population (Hardcastle, 1985; Rounds, 1988; Zellmer & Anderson-Meger, 2011). Rounds (1988) reports that "traditional" and "moral" rural attitudes are often grounded in more fundamental religious belief systems often deeply embedded within rural culture, and informal helping systems are more prominent in rural areas compared to urban communities. Similarly, Blank, Fox, Hargrove, and Turner (1995) found that there is a greater dependence on personal and family support among residents suffering from mental illness. Wagenfeld, Murray, Mohatt, and DeBruyn (1994) discussed issues associated with conservative ideologies held by rural residents and attitudes concerning drug and alcohol abuse. The authors caution "the generally more conservative climate in rural states might be reflected in reduced community tolerance for deviant behavior of drug abuse" (p. 19). The sociopolitical conservative nature of rural areas can be both a positive and a negative. It is positive in that it is a shared way in which a population comes to understand and interpret the spaces in which they live, work, and socialize. It is negative in the sense that these life views discourage discourse, limit options of response, and too often lead to a "blaming" approach to problem resolution. It can also create sociopolitical stress within a community.

Rural states are more likely to support and elect conservative officials over those identified as more liberal. Sociopolitically conservative officials in turn often support the "rugged individualist" mind-set and life ways of rural residents. They may argue that there is a need to reduce the federal government's role from local communities, but, at the same time, states that are dominated by agricultural concerns and those who represent them in Congress are typically reluctant to want support reduced for rural social and economic programs. For example, the Rural Electrification Administration was created in 1935 to assist in the process of bringing mass electricity to rural areas. Considered largely successful in supporting getting electricity across vast and remote areas of the United States, its mission was largely complete by the early 1970s. However, the agency remained intact until 1994 when its functions were assumed by the Rural Utilities Service, a component of the US Department of Agriculture (Rural Utilities Service, 2011). Other examples exist as well. One area of interest is often found in what is commonly referred to as "the Farm Bill" (USDA Farm Bill, 2011). This legislation is the primary agricultural and food policy of the US government and is a comprehensive omnibus bill that is reviewed approximately every five years by the US Congress. This legislation includes not only elements that support the production of agricultural and forest products, but rural economic development, international trade, commodity subsidies, transportation, food safety, and rural social programs as well. The Farm Bill contains and supports a considerable amount of social programming and community development—through public dollars. Rural residents who may otherwise not support government intervention and argue against government spending are at the same time direct or indirect recipients of government assistance provided through political mechanisms such as the Farm Bill.

The reality is that, at one level, many who live in rural places want to preserve their rugged individualism and independence, while, at the same time, they want to continue the federally supported subsidies and social programs that provide needed support to rural communities. This can create a challenge, especially among those from outside the "culture of rural." This uneasy relationship is further exacerbated when someone from outside a rural community (especially from an urban place) challenges this mind-set. For example, Professors Deborah and Frank Popper (1987) from New Jersey presented a conceptual proposal supporting the return of much of the high plains across the middle belt of the United States to natural prairie. This idea has come to be known commonly as the "buffalo commons," and part of the plan includes removing humans from a large portion of the landscape. This plan focused on reclaiming large areas of the American Great Plains from what they saw as failed expansion policies; expensive agricultural subsidization; the depletion of natural resources such as water, needed to irrigate marginal land; and land management practices that are unsustainable (Pedeliski, 2011). As you can imagine, those living on the prairie were not impressed. This was seen as an attack and affront to their way of life, yet another attempt to isolate and marginalize a population, and, perhaps worst of all, coming from what they saw as overeducated, arrogant, outsiders from of all places, the Eastern Seaboard—a place full of people who never even tried to understand the prairie or the people on it. This is not to say that Popper and Popper were necessarily wrong. All of the problems they identified are real and continue to exist: shrinking populations, federal and state costs that could never be recouped, economic challenges, and failing communities. To the Poppers, these places are ripe for returning to a more natural state. They argued that the federal government should buy out those still there, reseed the land with native grasses, and essentially return it to the bison, thus becoming a "buffalo commons." However, what was not considered were the human elements embedded deep in the culture of those living there—the churches, community centers, ranches, and family histories, as well as the history of a country itself. As you can see, this was an example of how something can appear to be a good idea but fails to recognize the broader scope and value of things less tangible but no less important.

Rural social workers must be aware of and understand conflicts such as what we learned from the buffalo commons example to be effective. In fact, it is possible—even likely—that a social worker in a rural area is supported by public money to perform their duties from a rural social program initiative, meaning they themselves are viewed to varying degrees as agents acting on behalf of a government entity. As such, some community members may view them as outsiders because they are affiliated with what is seen as a representative of external control. Often this is an area best avoided in discussions in the community. When the discussion must be broached, it is best to be honest and remain focused on responsibilities of the position and not on an individual. Social workers can be seen both positively and negatively in any community, but this is amplified in rural areas. Negatively, the social worker can be viewed as a part of the "government process," a member of a system that represents external control over a population. Positively, a social worker can be an active participant with a community and work to respond to and address local or regional concerns. In a sense, the rural social worker must be many things to many people: the child welfare worker and the grant writer for new playground equipment, the mental health care provider to an aging population, and the catalyst for developing a rural transportation program for elderly residents. Understanding the complexities of sociopolitical processes in rural areas can be challenging.

Dr. Michael Rosmann, a clinical psychologist and farmer in western Iowa, discusses understanding rural culture (specifically among farmers) in his book *Excellent Joy: Fishing, Farming, Hunting, and Psychology* (2011). According to Rosmann, the behavioral culture of farmers is best understood through an understanding of the land upon which they live. He states that "ownership of a family farm is the triumphant result of the struggles of multiple generations of immigrants to America" (p. 142), and to lose the farm is seen as bringing shame on the family. Further, the loss of a farm is seen as a broken covenant with future generations who could have otherwise maintained the family tradition. In more urban or suburban areas when someone is no longer able to pay for his or her house, the effects can be painful, costly, and embarrassing. But in urbanized areas people are more likely to move more often and "move up" as resources allow. Among rural and farming cultures, a house is often more than just a home; it is an identity and one that defines an entire clan of people, not just one family unit or an individual. Rosmann summarizes this behavioral concept well by stating that, ultimately, "the emotional well-being of family farmers is intimately entwined with this way of life" (p. 142). This emotional attachment to the past, present, as well as the future can take its toll. Pressures from external forces such as the environment, commodity prices, overhead costs, and the community can create a sense of little control over one's own place. Too little rain, too much rain, low commodity prices, and high operating costs are all beyond the control of a farmer. Behaviorally speaking, this can be devastating. Rosmann (2011) shares that as a psychologist he would often receive telephone calls from people scared, embarrassed, and ashamed of their situation. The caller would want to initiate contact to seek help. As a fellow farmer, they felt more comfortable calling him because he could better understand their situation. This is an important cultural element among rural communities that cannot be overstated. A rural social worker does not necessarily need to be a farmer or a factory worker or even from the area in which they work, but it does help. There is a sense of connectedness that increases comfort among rural dwellers—a connectedness that likely stems from a cultural lifestyle that often favors "informal" rather than "formal" helping systems. Rural areas are isolated by the very nature of space that they occupy. As a result, there is a historic and traditional helping system already built into the community. Therefore, there is a greater dependence on more informal approaches to helping.

So how does a rural social worker not from the area in which he or she works develop the type of trust necessary to facilitate greater support and participation? When one is not from the area, and especially if he or she is from a more urbanized place, it is important to "become" part of the community in ways that are appropriate. For example, coaching youth sports, attending a church of choice, becoming involved with school boards, and serving on county or township committees can all be highly valuable and enhance the integration of the social worker into the broader context of the community. At the same time, the rural social worker must always be cognizant of the challenge of "dual relationships" where the two worlds cross. Imagine that you are coaching your daughter's youth soccer team and one of the other children on the team is a member of a client's family. In rural areas this happens—a lot. Sound social work ethics come into play here, and there is a way to balance the two worlds. The social worker must not, of course, talk about what he or she knows about the family and, at the same time, be able to show how he or she can separate between the two worlds. It can be a challenge, but it is necessary to be both effective and accepted. The cultural process of rural places makes it necessary that the social worker maintain this balance between personal and professional spaces.

Not unlike what one finds in urban communities, rural communities have a strong sense of understanding and appreciation for the family unit. What is somewhat different among rural residents regarding families is how they are socially constructed and the expectations placed on individuals as members of a group rather than as individuals alone. Refer back to the discussion by Rosmann (2011) regarding the interconnectedness among farm families. Here, the family unit is seen as having a direct link from the past through the present to the future, grounded in the collective and shared experience of the land and the homestead. This cultural interpretation of how families best operate is not altogether different from what is found in rural areas more generally. While most people living in rural areas do not actively farm, many identify with the farm culture and life way. To try and better understand the distinction between the life ways of those living in rural versus urban areas, a review of Tonnies's (1963) sociological work on the differences between the concepts "Gemeinschaft" and "Geselleschaft" may provide a deeper understanding. Tonnies defines *Gemeinschaft* as that which focuses on influences of the local or regional community onto the family unit, and *Geselleschaft*, as that which places greater emphasis on the influences of the broader society. The distinction between the two concepts is important to understanding rural and urban family differences. Generally speaking, rural families and the individuals who are included in these units are more heavily influenced by *Gemeinschaft*, whereas more urbanized dwellers are more likely to be influenced by *Geselleschaft* as that. Essentially, the satisfaction of life is more associated with the influences of the community and social norms that reside in these communities among rural residents, but among urban residents, the influences of the greater society and social norms that are derived from it are more important (Panelli, 2006). Assuming this is an accurate assessment, it makes sense given the regional isolation rural places inherently experience. The broader society, that which is seen on television, from the movies, or the Internet, is often literally many miles away. Images, lifestyles, and behaviors exhibited from these places are abstract in that they are almost never born from rural places. They are not immediately familiar. In more urbanized areas, these images are more familiar, perhaps even stemming from that or a similar urban scape. Socio-cultural influences, be it lifestyle, behavior, clothing, music, or politics, ultimately come from somewhere, and to those living in rural places, that somewhere is usually somewhere else.

This information may help the rural social worker understand how and why rural populations may interpret themselves, and why they sometimes make the decisions they do. For example, in a more urbanized area it may be considered more acceptable to admit that an individual is experiencing an addiction and in need of treatment services. There may simply be a cultural tolerance among urban residents that is higher than what is found in rural communities. But to settle on this explanation alone is to oversimplify the problem. For example, we know that rural residents are less likely to have access to drug or alcohol treatments due to the lack of resources as well as social acceptability and rural conservatism (Conger, 1997). It is commonplace that rural health care facilities lack detoxification or psychiatric services, and too often jails are used to monitor those who may otherwise have been better served by more advanced services (Cellucci, Vik, & Nirenberg, 2003). However, what we do not yet fully understand is how to best address the problem. The rural social worker is challenged by this reality. Cellucci, Vik, and Nirenberg (2003) suggest one of the most effective approaches to this type of health concern in rural areas is to adopt a public health model of intervention, to be proactive and work with a community to identify problem areas before rates of addiction and abuse escalate. In addition, these authors suggest that there is a need to create collaborations between public and private service providers and funders to effectively distribute treatment options as well as costs. Centralized service provision does not best respond to the needs of a population scattered across broad landscapes. Finally, they suggest that there is a great need for better research on the root causes of addictions in rural areas and treatments in these environments. They recognize that at this time it is difficult to draw concrete conclusions regarding the unique challenges of addictions in rural areas given the overall lack of knowledge and understanding about the problem.

Regardless of whether we are discussing the challenges associated with addictions, mental illness, or community development in rural areas, it is impossible to fully address the concerns until there is a sound understanding about how the effects of rural sociocultural realities impact the discussion. It's not that the direct practice treatment of an individual is any different in rural areas compared to urban ones. A clinical social worker practicing cognitive behavioral therapy (CBT) in a rural area will follow the same practice guidelines and treatment approaches as they would if they were working in an urban area—CBT is CBT. There is no rural CBT or urban CBT. That said, how the treatment is administered may be altered or influenced by how the community perceives it, or, more accurately, how the individual perceives it in the context of how the community interprets seeking therapy. As Rosmann (2011) stated, it's not that farmers did not want to seek help, they did. But first they wanted and needed to build a trust in the provider; they needed to believe that the provider had a sense of their problems and could understand them. They wanted help and sought it out—but only after certain sociocultural elements were satisfied.

ETHICAL CONSIDERATIONS AND CONCERNS IN RURAL AREAS

The body of literature on rural behavioral health and social service practice is well lined with discussions pertaining to ethical considerations. Ethics as defined by the Code of Ethics by the National Association of Social Workers (2013) is the same document regardless of where one practices. However, different ethical considerations must be addressed when working in rural areas. Challenges associated with this topic are essentially inverted between rural and urban locations, meaning whereas urban areas are densely populated in smaller space, rural areas are more sparsely populated across more open landscape—but people tend to travel to and congregate in similar spaces. In a city, where perhaps millions of people live, one may very well separate themselves from those they serve merely by living a few miles away or in a different but nearby municipality. Here the social worker will eat in different restaurants, shop in different clothing and grocery stores, live in different school districts, and attend different churches. In rural areas, people from broader distances will shop at the same grocery store, live in the same school district, and attend the same church. In short, a social worker in a rural community is much more likely to see clients in public, be recognized as a professional, and otherwise ironically live a more public life than her or his counterparts in more urban places.

As one can imagine, the ethical challenges associated with the complex nature of dual relationships can be difficult to navigate. The best way to approach these challenges is to be ever conscious of the reality that in rural areas, you will interact with clients outside of your practice and people often know or at least know of each other. To illustrate, imagine that you live in a large, sprawling, metropolitan area and work on the other side of the city. Due to regional differences such as different socioeconomics between you and your clients, different areas where one works and shops, and other differences between populations, one could in theory talk about a client (though this would be highly unethical, unprofessional, and potentially illegal) with another person who will never (beyond random chance) meet any of your clients. In rural areas, the situation is completely reversed. Here, the likelihood of someone you know knowing someone in your care increases exponentially. Therefore, there is an even greater need to maintain confidentiality and, in addition, be aware of how confidentiality can be compromised even in unlikely ways.

An example of this is represented by one of this book's authors. While working in a remote part of the United States and on a Native American reservation, it became obvious that regardless of how careful the social worker was to try and maintain confidentiallity in the community, it was brought to the social worker's attention that a community member learned of a family receiving services. When asked how the person would know, the response was, "Your work van was seen parked in their yard a few days ago." This is a good example of how well people often know each other's activities in a rural area. Knowing that there was little one could do about the vehicle the social worker drove, there may have been no other response in this particular case. However, there are strategies one can employ. In this particular case, the family and social worker discussed this as a potential issue associated with these services. The family recognized this as a concern and agreed to meet at the hospital for future sessions. While their car could be recognized in the hospital parking lot, there was a higher level of other plausible explanations for it being there (seeking health care services or visiting a sick friend or relative, for example). As you can see, rural social workers must work to anticipate possible ethical dilemmas and challenges regularly and seek to minimize the possible impact of these dilemmas the best they can.

Another issue that sometimes arises in rural areas is challenges associated with knowing the client at a much more personal level that one might otherwise find comfortable. Given that social workers are often from the area where they live and even grew up, eventually there will be a situation where you will know community members all too well—sometimes they are even relatives. While this is best approached on a case-by-case basis, it is usually good to maintain sound ethical practices in situations such as these. Too often the conventional response is to contact the social worker's supervisor and ask that the case be transferred to someone else. While this is a reasonable response and one that is often used, sometimes that isn't an option as you might be the only person able to help. Unfortunately, there is no "right" answer here, and the best advice is to contact a supervisor, coworker, or colleague and discuss the problem further. Do not feel like you have to make the decision alone.

CULTURAL COMPETENCE AND SPECIAL POPULATIONS IN RURAL AREAS

Rural areas of the United States are often seen as largely homogeneous, and dominated by ethnically European-descent populations. While this is often the case, it is also becoming less so over time, and more non-white populations of people reside in rural areas. But this is not necessarily a new phenomenon. Large populations of Hispanic and Latino and Latina communities have long lived in the southwestern United States, and large and even majority populations of African Americans live across the southern United States. Native Americans live across large areas of the western and prairie states, as well as across the northern Midwest. But in many respects, these are nearly stereotypical statements. While everyone knows that large populations of Native Americans live in South Dakota, Oklahoma, and Alaska, and there is a high concentration of African Americans in Alabama, Mississippi, and Georgia, it is important to recognize and understand that diverse populations live everywhere in the United States—in all states. For rural social workers, it is paramount to the success of their ability to practice to understand the need to be culturally competent and understanding of the unique life ways of special populations.

In rural areas specifically, there is a growth in diversity. For example, in the 1970s the United States accepted a large refugee population of Hmong from Vietnam. This group of people were allies of the US government during the Vietnam conflict and, as a result, in need of a "safe harbor" away from their war torn nation. Many came to the United States and settled in rural areas. Later, and as a result of the conflicts in Somalia and Sudan, refugees again came to the United States seeking refuge. Not unlike the Hmong, many settled in rural areas. As one can imagine (or for those from these special populations, fully understand), moves such as this represented great challenge.

In isolated areas where anonymity is essentially nonexistent, new groups of culturally diverse people are noticed. They bring new cultural values, norms, and mores, and they seek to be fully accepted into their new surroundings. This can be challenging anywhere, but in rural areas more so due to the lower populations of people in general. Challenges associated with new groups of people immigrating to the United States include issues pertaining to understanding local or indigenous norms, language, education, employment, and religion, and even more pedestrian issues such as shopping, participating in extracurricular and social activities, or buying a house.

While it is important to recognize and focus on challenges faced by ethnic or religious subpopulations, it is equally important to not overlook other, less noticeable groups as well. For example, the unique circumstances surrounding military personnel since the attacks of 9/11 created unanticipated issues in rural areas. The wars in Iraq and Afghanistan were supported by large numbers of soldiers, sailors, members of the Air Force, and Marines serving in rural National Guard and Reserve units. As a result, many rural residents in military service returned from active duty deployments to rural and small communities across America. For those who sustained injuries, access to care is grossly underrepresented in rural areas, with most Veterans Affairs hospitals and mental health care facilities located in more urban locations. As a result of this disconnect, many rural Veterans in need of services find it difficult to access timely and adequate care (Mackie, 2012).

Another subpopulation in rural areas of great concern is the poor, specifically, poor families. It is tragic to find families living in poverty anywhere, and in rural areas it becomes more pronounced with the challenges associated with access to services, availability of employment, and ability to secure other basic necessities. Poverty knows no single population, but too often it is the children who struggle the most. Rural social workers are responsible to recognize and address the unique concerns related to this and all other underrepresented populations.

Social workers in rural areas are in the unique position to assist those who may be new to the area as well as the culture. Here is where social workers can shine the brightest through their ability to bridge between cultures, develop and support inclusion activities, and otherwise show leadership in the community. A social worker by the very nature of their education is expected to serve as an advocate and champion for diversity. In rural areas this is a skill often needed, not necessarily because of the painful realities associated with racism (though it is fair to acknowledge that racism exists everywhere, including rural areas), but from a strengths-based, human-centered perspective where all are treated equally and all receive equal access. The rural social worker needs to be constantly aware of the need to educate, inform, and address the needs of cultural differences and be prepared to place themselves in the conversations that occur.

GLOBALIZATION AND THE IMPACT ON RURAL PLACES

Globalization, be it about economics, immigration, or politics, is a complex topic to address and certainly well beyond the scope of this text. But to not at least acknowledge the impacts of globalization in rural areas of the United States would be a mistake. Rural areas are currently being impacted by events occurring across the globe—and while some impacts are positive, they are too often negative with harmful consequences for rural residents.

For the purposes of the context of this book, globalization is defined as economic and intellectual activities that exchange goods and services across large spaces. Through the use of advanced technology, globalization allows marketplace stakeholders to engage in relationships where opportunities are maximized and abundant, prices are cheapest, or operations can be most efficiently and effectively managed. The concept of globalization is certainly not new. Across history, globalization existed (even when it wasn't actually global). An example of this is in the Silk Road trading between central Asia and Europe in the middle ages. In colonial America, global trade was the economic bedrock of early settlements. Goods, services, and labor were transported from Europe to the colonies and sold or bartered. In return, goods that were either found in the New World or better suited to growth and development there were exchanged back to Europe and elsewhere. Globalization today is in some ways much the same, but also very different.

Today, globalization combined with the ability to efficiently transport goods and services has changed how economic exchanges work, and is what some now refer to as the flat earth (this term refers to the idea that the world is "flattening" due to advances in communication, technology, and transportation where information, goods, and services are more easily exchanged and distributed around the globe), which is an extension of the concepts presented by Thomas L. Friedman in the book *The World Is Flat: A Brief History of the 21st Century* (2005). Here, Friedman argues that a series of technological and economic events ultimately contributed to creating an environment where goods and services can be and are exchanged across the globe, with the goal of maximizing opportunity and growth. In rural areas (especially in the midwestern region of the United States), we see the effects of globalization in nearly every corner of society. Rural areas are unique in that, at some point, many have benefited from these concepts. For example, instead of the "Big Three" automobile companies manufacturing all components necessary to assemble a car in Detroit, companies were born that produced some of the parts, shipped them to the factory (usually in the Detroit area but not always), and it was there that the vehicle was assembled. Imagine how this worked: A set of wiring harnesses that connect to the headlamps were made in Akron, the headlamp itself was made in Flint, the tires were made in Dayton, and the wheel hubs made in Fort Wayne. When parts were needed, calls were made, orders placed, and trucks hauled these parts to the main factory to assemble the car. While not rural, per se, these "feeder" manufacturing plants employed people in places far from the assembly plant and contributed to the economies of smaller regional cities and surrounding areas. Over time, opportunities to manufacture these components cheaper were found in other nations, be they in China, Mexico, or Estonia. Because of faster and more dependable technology, communication issues became less of a concern. And due to more careful inventory processing coupled with transportation, parts could be shipped from nearly anywhere in the world quickly and affordably. In short, manufacturers were no longer bound to needing their suppliers in the same geographic proximity as they had been in the past. This in turn has created new economic opportunities in some places but contributed to challenges in others. Rural areas of the United States where feeder factories were located have, in many ways, struggled to maintain relevancy and further limited employment opportunities where they once existed.

While globalization has been interpreted as a paradigm where one can successfully gather goods, services, and resources from a variety of places around the world, Friedman (2005) argues that this does not need to be the only approach to creating efficiencies, and that these processes can be achieved within a single nation, especially one as large and dynamic as the United States. To illustrate: A call center for a banking or customer service firm can be located in areas where labor is abundant, the cost of living (and thus, cost of operations) is lower, and the focus is on the strengths of a community. There may not be a need to move a company to a faraway land when opportunities exist within a county's own borders. An example of this is found in less populated places where an educated and ready workforce exists, such as found often in prairie, midwestern, or southern states of the United States. Often more rural in nature, these are regions and places where postmodern economies have replaced past industrial and agricultural economies, but educated and available labor forces continue to exist. Looking at globalization from this perspective is to actually apply what globalization is and, at the same time, seek ways to strengthen areas where economic weaknesses currently exist.

GLOBALIZATION AND RURAL SOCIAL WORK PRACTICE

It has long been recognized that economically healthy communities are always the goal, and too often rural areas lack economic stability today. However, it is becoming increasingly important to recognize that rural areas do contain certain attributes not necessarily found in other areas of the United States. For example, the rural Midwest is an excellent place to grow food crops and animals, harvest lumber products, and conduct mining operations. It is also a place where highly developed and respected colleges and universities are located. Along the same vein, the Rocky Mountain states have the unique distinction of being places where people want to be and live, largely due to the landscape and opportunities for recreation. This is also a region rich in timber as a natural resource. The same can be said for areas in the South, as these are areas where natural resources exist and places where certain crops can be grown more efficiently than in other parts of the United States. These of course are positive attributes. It can also be said that there are negative attributes across these largely rural regions as well. Mountain states may be great places for ski resorts, but they are no longer places where mining dominates the economic landscape as it did in the past. The Midwest, once known as the center of the industrial complex, the miller of grains, and builder of cars, no longer finds these as staple economic drivers. The economics of the southern United States was once largely focused on agriculture, but on agricultural products that are either less in demand today or cheaper to produce elsewhere.

The rural social worker of today needs to be able to identify strengths in communities to better be able to help, and understanding the effects of globalization is important in this process. Too often, there are examples of how rural residents want things to remain as they were or, if the economic landscape has changed (and for most, it has), to return to a world where opportunities existed (Longworth, 2008). But this is likely not to be, and as controversial as the idea may be to some, likely shouldn't be pursued, as past economic processes failed for a reason—they simply didn't work any longer. Instead, the rural social worker can work to help develop new approaches to addressing rural needs based on an understanding of how economic processes work, and an ability to focus on strengths, not weaknesses, in a region. To illustrate, across the Midwest and the western United States there are now several places where one can find wind and solar electricity generation plants. This is an example of how a geographic area is maximizing the resources it has available. Placing these facilities in areas like New England or elsewhere is either uneconomical or at least not as advantageous as where they are now. These places in turn create opportunities for labor in the manufacturing, erecting, and maintaining of the facilities. But we also know that members of the community must have "buy-in" as these are not places where one can simply exploit. Ultimately, it requires a community's collective focus and goals associated with developing new economies and identifying strength areas to be successful. It is equally important to remember the history, heritage, and background of the people living in a particular area. These sociocultural aspects are also important in understanding what can be done, how it can be accomplished, and in what ways ambitions can be achieved. There is a place here for the social worker to actively engage in this conversation, as these are the professionally prepared community members who have studied and thought carefully about how systems work with and around each other, and how to maximize capital and potential.

CONCLUSION

While it is impossible to discuss all of the specific ethnocultural concerns related to all different groups living in rural areas, it is possible to address the concerns from a broad perspective and prepare rural social workers to be conscientious, consistent, and respectful to the needs of others. Focusing on the needs of specific populations is important for empowering people, both the new populations living in rural places as well as those who claim longer-term residency. The social worker is uniquely positioned to work toward developing programs as well as relationships that enhance living conditions and diversity throughout the community. Human diversity across rural areas is becoming more complex and, thus, often creates challenges for communities that were unprepared and sometimes unwilling to embrace the changes that occurred. Examples include an influx of groups who may speak languages other than English or practice religions that differ from those more commonly practiced in the region. These are, however, opportunities for communities to change and grow. Rural areas (especially in the United States) have a long and rich history of being places where immigration occurs, and where people can find new opportunities to grow. Social workers in these places have the unique ability to serve as conduits between cultures, to foster communication and collaboration, and to focus on newly defined needs in positive ways. Because they are embedded in the local community, they will also likely hold unique knowledge about the life ways and culture of the area from a historical vantage point. Together, they can work between, among, and within the varying systems to identify and encourage positive outcomes.

Globalization is not always a concept readily attributed to rural concerns, but it should be. The effects of globalization of economies have had an important impact on rural areas across all systems levels. Rural communities once could focus on a single industry or economic driver to sustain the labor force. With many of those industries either gone or downsized today, many wonder what if anything can be done. Here again, rural social workers are prepared to address social problems across a variety of systems levels and are prepared to identify areas of strength and weakness, at the micro, mezzo, and macro levels. Having a basic understanding of how globalization has impacted rural areas is a good start, but it's not enough. The social worker should continue to learn and develop an even deeper understanding about how to identify community strengths and focus on ways to improve rural communities.

The rural social worker is uniquely skilled in being able to see social problems from a broad perspective and then facilitate positive, sustainable change. While most workers would not start an economic venture, they can help facilitate the process through their knowledge of how economics connects with social welfare, especially from a macro systems perspective. While improving the economics of a rural community does not impact specific behavioral health needs per se, as that falls into the micro realm, it is an important component to the overall health and quality of life in rural places.

Related Websites and Other Resources (for Further Learning Opportunities, Discussion Questions)

- https://www.childwelfare.gov/preventing/developing/rural_communities.cfm. This website links one to the US Department of Health and Human Services Child Welfare Information Gateway and provides a variety of information related to cultural competence in rural practice, especially among family and child services.
- https://www.raconline.org/topics/workforce-education-and-training/websites-tools. This website links to information on culturally competent practices from the Rural Assistance Center. Here, one can find definitions of cultural competence from a rural perspective, how to practice more competently in rural areas, and how to train and educate staff in being more culturally aware and competent.

6

Looking Forward

WHERE IS RURAL SOCIAL WORK GOING FROM HERE?

The need for social workers practicing in rural areas will continue to be in demand. As we now know, the overall population of rural and isolated areas is growing older as more of the youths leave and those who continue to live in these areas age. Given the aging rural population, now more than ever there is a need for rural social workers to develop skills and knowledge in gerontology and commit to the care of the elderly on the micro level. Beginning now and spanning into the foreseeable future, there will be an increased need for social workers to be actively engaged in the wider variety of needs associated with rural elderly populations and unique circumstances challenging this group. From a macro perspective, as the rural population ages, there will be even higher needs for people to be able to access affordable and appropriate housing, transportation, and health care. These are not small issues in rural areas. Transportation, housing, and health care all present unique challenges to all who live in rural places. However, for the elderly, these challenges will only increase as communities seek new and dynamic ways to respond to a shifting demographic.

Recognizing the needs of rural elderly is important, but that is not to say that there are no other populations of concern as well. For example, children and youths in rural areas also present unique needs. When compared to more urban counterparts, residents in

134

rural areas are more likely to experience poverty and rural communities often have lower tax bases, meaning schools may be more stressed to meet the budgetary demand to provide education and support for children and youths. As the rural population ages, the youths will become more vulnerable and in need of more dynamic solutions to respond to education needs. School social workers are professionals who will hold special knowledge about the needs of children in rural areas ranging from the challenges associated with education, to mental and physical health, to family and community needs. These social workers will be asked to be more creative than ever before in their contribution to developing micro, mezzo, and macro interventions.

On a much more macro level, rural social workers can make significant contributions to problems and issues associated with rural social and economic development. Social development includes a wide variety of concerns, including working with community members to identify and address community needs. As a professional guild, social workers are astutely aware of community needs and can provide informed, educated, and compassionate insights to developing social infrastructure that benefits and enhances the rural community. For example, a social worker in a rural area can provide education and support around understanding the processes associated with human rights, population needs, public funding, and advocacy for change. Here is where rural social workers can be highly effective. Often, funding for local and regional social service programs is directed through county political entities. A well-informed social worker can and should become familiar with how a variety of systems are funded, build the relationship capital to work with a variety of stakeholders, and provide valuable information that serves to provide the best services available in a place where resources are almost always very limited.

Another area of notable concern across rural areas is that of diversity (Summers, 1998). No differently than in more populated areas, human diversity is broad and far reaching. In rural areas, this diversity is often defined not only by vulnerable populations (such as the elderly or children) but as cultural and ethnic diversity as well. Specifically, due to labor needs in agricultural communities, large populations of immigrant workers are often overrepresented in the population but underrepresented in the social and political processes of the community. Problems manifest in lack of adequate support in schools to address language barriers, isolation in the community between specific groups, and challenges associated with accessing basic services such as social welfare support or even law enforcement. For example, imagine if a family who has members who are illegally residing in the United States are in need of child welfare services. A social worker may find herself caught between a sense of responsibility to provide assistance and, at the same time, a feeling of responsibility to comply with laws requiring that law enforcement or the courts be notified of either the need for services or even the existence of someone who is living in the country illegally. Regardless of where one falls in this ongoing and colossal debate around immigration in the United States, a rural social worker may well find themselves caught in an ethical dilemma between providing services and serving as a general member of the community.

In rural areas of the United States, Native Americans represent a diverse group with large populations. In many areas (especially in the western United States but anywhere in the country) rural social workers should expect to work with members of Native American communities. This creates a unique set of challenges and opportunities given the sovereign political nature of these communities with the federal government. Unlike other ethnic populations, Native Americans have special status with regard to laws and policies, largely grounded in treaties and similar agreements with the US federal government. Practicing among Native American populations is unique in that, often, laws and jurisdictions that are drawn from a state government do not necessarily apply, and one must learn the applicability of tribal and federal laws within this specific context. For example, The Indian Child Welfare Act of 1977 was created as federal law to provide child and family protection that is unique to Native American communities. Child protection workers must be fully conscious of these laws, or risk violating federally regulated rights. Rural social workers practicing in and near indigenous communities must be prepared to further their learning and broaden their experiences in the areas of culture, law, and policy.

WHAT ROLES CAN SOCIAL WORKERS PLAY IN THE FUTURE OF RURAL ENVIRONMENTS?

Social workers are in demand across rural America in a wide variety of areas of practice. Rural areas are no different than urban areas in that people are people wherever one goes, and social service needs do not differ in the sense that services are services. However, what is different in rural areas may perhaps be best described as problems associated with access and challenges associated with culture. In rural areas, transportation issues are often more extreme that in urban places given the challenges associated with the distance that defines rural. With access, challenges abound be they access to health care and mental health care, education, employment, and even basic necessities such as groceries. But access is not just about geographic space—it is cultural as well. The practice of rural social work can be different because the culture of rural is often different when compared to more populated and urbanized places. In rural locations (generally speaking), residents sometimes view agents of the government as outsiders and, typically, social workers operate as agents of the county or state. They have access to information, knowledge, groups, and processes that may raise suspicion or concern. They often represent governmental power be it as a child protection worker or provider of health and human services. Even if community members claim to understand what a social worker does and expect them to do their job (whatever that job may be), the social worker will still likely find accessing the life ways of rural communities to be potentially challenging (Daley, 2015). It is important to understand that it can take time to allow a community to grow to know you and develop the trust needed to be fully effective. In urban areas, anonymity is not uncommon and even expected. In rural areas it's often just the opposite—anonymity is viewed as a bad thing and preference is given to knowing someone, which is to say, knowing about things others may find personal such as political affiliations, church preferences, marital status, and other information. For many rural residents, this is information needed to evaluate and assess others' places in society. A rural social worker is in a precarious place in that, to be accepted, there is a need to share some information and "have a history" within the community while, at the same time, remaining objective and neutral. This said, one must become part of the community to be able to fully access the community. It's a delicate balance to create and then maintain.

The rural social worker is well poised to participate in a wide variety of roles in the future of rural areas. By design, undergraduate-educated social workers are prepared as generalists and, as such, have been educated to work in a wide variety of systems. Perhaps more important to rural social workers, there is a need for those practicing in isolated areas and small communities to be flexible, creative, and willing to work across systems, often times simultaneously. This, of course, applies to those prepared for the field at the master-level as well. However, a graduate-level prepared social worker will likely have been trained in some form of specialty. While this is not, nor should it be viewed as, a limitation, applying a more generalist approach to service delivery can be advantageous to successful rural practice. For example, a child protection social worker in a rural area will be aware of unique problems that may contribute to child maltreatment. At one level, there will need to be a micro-level response, which may be defined as the need for individual intervention in the name of a child or family. At the mezzo level, that same child may be negatively impacted by the lack of supports from extended family or local community, and at the macro level, the social worker may identify broader socioeconomic problems associated with the initial case. Here, the social worker will be highly astute and knowledgeable about a variety of social needs and be able to propose a variety of responses to these challenges. Perhaps more important is the transformative effect a rural social worker can have on a rural community. Because of their unique knowledge, rural social workers can work with a variety of stakeholders to address a plethora of social concerns.

IS RURAL SOCIAL WORK PRACTICE FOR YOU?

Rural social work practice is, for many very good reasons, not for everyone. Perhaps most important, working in a rural or otherwise isolated place requires at some level an interest in and appreciation for rural lifestyle and culture. These are also places that favor independence and the ability to solve complex problems with limited resources. They are also places where one must be regularly creative in daily practice, how they maintain continuing education, and discover opportunities that may otherwise go overlooked. In short, living in a rural place is simply different from more populated areas, and it's important to be comfortable with that unchangeable truth. There is no assumption that to be a good social worker, one must have grown up in a rural area. However, research has shown that those who grew up in rural areas are more likely to return to work in rural areas (Mackie, 2007, 2012). This is not to imply that to be a rural social worker one must have grown up in a rural area, only that those who do so often have roots in the rural experience. Evidence also suggests that students who complete a practicum in a rural area and were exposed to rural knowledge and practice content are also more likely to consider practicing in rural areas (Mackie, 2007). What is likely most important is that to be successful, social workers in rural areas must be genuinely interested in becoming part of the community, living a rural lifestyle, and be willing to become a part of the rural fabric.

For those from rural areas, the process of integrating into the rural lifestyle is already embedded. For those not as familiar with rural life ways, it is important to become involved in the community, which can be done in a variety of ways, such as joining community-based organizations such as the Jaycees, Lions, or other fraternal or civic clubs. Attending the church of your choice will also help in the process of integrating into the community. While it seems cliché, it can be highly beneficial to become engaged with the community at the community level, and learn about the nuances of where one lives.

Perhaps at the end of the conversation about whether or not one is to become a rural social worker are simple but straightforward questions—is this how and where you want to live and work? Is this where you want to raise a family? Is this professionally rewarding? Do the qualities associated with rural living outweigh those things often identified with living in a more urbanized location (social activities, restaurants, and cultural events)? Too often, these authors (all of whom have practiced in rural places) noted how sometimes the fantasy of rural life becomes blurred with the reality. For one author, in particular, it was often noticed how people from more urbanized locations would visit an area in the northern United States on vacation during the summer and "fall in love" with the region. Because of this, they would later move there only to find the challenges associated with eight months of winter, the long distances between places and resources, the very real and chronic poverty in outlying communities, and the overall lack of services (which can be frustrating). Not fully understanding the challenges of the life ways of the local communities, they would later leave frustrated and disheartened. Yes, rural areas allow for a wide variety of opportunities and, for rural social workers, the challenges and joys attached to providing care for people in need, but, at the end of this discussion, you have to ultimately decide if working in a rural area is right for you.

RECOMMENDED READINGS

Carlton-LaNey, I. B., Edwards, R. L., & Reid, P. N. (Eds.) (1999). *Preserving and strengthening small towns and rural communities.* Washington, DC: NASW Press.

Carr, P. J., & Kefalas, M. J. (2009). *Hollowing out the middle: The rural brain drain and what it means to America.* Boston: Beacon Press.

Chank, J. A., & Skovholt, T. M. (2006). *Ethical practice in small communities: Challenges and rewards for psychologists.* Washington, DC: American Psychological Association Press.

Collier, K. (2006). *Social work with rural peoples* (3rd ed.). Vancouver, BC: New Star Books.

Daley, M. R. (2015). *Rural social work in the 21st century.* Chicago, IL: Lyceum Books, Inc.

Donehower, K., Hogg, C., & Scheel, E. E. (2007). *Rural literacies.* Carbondale, IL: Southern Illinois University Press.

Flora, C. B., Flora, J. L., & Fey, S. (2004). *Rural communities: Legacy + Change* (2nd ed.). Boulder, CO: Westview Press.

Ginsberg, L. H. (Ed.) (1998). *Social work in rural communities* (3rd ed.). Washington, DC: CSWE Press.

Ginsberg, L. H. (Ed.) (2005). *Social work in rural communities* (4th ed.). Alexandria, VA: CSWE Press.

Ginsberg, L. H. (Ed.) (2011). *Social work in rural communities* (5th ed.). Alexandria, VA: CSWE Press.

Lohmann, N., & Lohmann, R. A. (Eds.) (2005). *Rural social work practice.* New York: Columbia University Press.

Martinez-Brawley, E. E. (2000). *Close to home: Human services and the small community.* Washington, DC: NASW Press.

Rosmann, M. R. (2011). *Excellent joy: Fishing, farming, hunting, and psychology.* North Liberty, IA: Ice Cube Books.

Scales, T. L., & Streeter, C. L. (Eds.) (2004). *Rural social work: Building and sustaining community assets.* Belmont, CA: Thompson Brooks/Cole Learning.

Stamm, B. H. (2003). *Rural behavioral health care: An interdisciplinary guide.* Washington, DC: American Psychological Association Press.

Weber, B. A., Duncan, G. J., & Whitener, L. A. (Eds.) (2003). *Rural dimensions of welfare reform.* Kalamazoo, MI: W. E. Upjohn Institute for Employment Research.

References

Alinsky, S. (1971). *Rules for radicals: A pragmatic primer for realistic radicals*. New York: Random House.

American Psychiatric Association. (2013). *Diagnostic and statistical manual of mental disorders* (5th ed.). Washington, DC: Author.

Anderson, D. B., & Shaw, S. (1994). Starting a support group for families and partners of people with HIV/AIDS in a rural setting. *Social Work, 39(1),* 135–138.

Andrews, J. (1987). A support group for rural women survivors of domestic violence. *Human Services in the Rural Environment, 1(2),* 39–42.

Appleby, G. A., Colon, E., & Hamilton, J. (2007). *Diversity, oppression, and social functioning: Person-in-environment assessment and intervention* (2nd ed.). Boston: Pearson/Allyn and Bacon.

Barker, R. L. (2004). *The social work dictionary* (5th ed.). Washington, DC: NASW Press.

Beck, E. L., & Eichler, M. (2000). Consensus organizing: A practice model for community building. *Journal of Community Practice, 8(1),* 87–102.

Blakley, T. L., & Mehr, N. (2008). Common ground: The development of a support group for survivors of homicide loss in a rural community. *Social Work with Groups, 31(3),* 239–254.

Blank, M. B., Fox, J. C., Hargrove, D. S., & Turner, J. T. (1995). Critical issues in reforming rural mental health service delivery. *Community Mental Health Journal, 31,* 511–523.

Brown, J. C. (1933). *The rural community and social case work.* New York: J. J. Little & Ives Company.

Carlton-LaNey, I. B., Edwards, R. L., & Reid, P. N. (1999). *Preserving and strengthening small towns and rural communities.* Washington, DC: NASW Press.

Carr, P. J., & Kefalas, M. J. (2009). *Hollowing out the middle: The rural brain drain and what it means for America.* Boston: Beacon Press.

Cashwell, S., & Just, M. M. (2008). Rural social work practice. In D. M. DiNitto & C. A. McNeese (Eds.), *Social work: Issues and opportunities in a challenging profession*. Chicago: Lyceum Books.

Cellucci, T., Vik, P., & Nirenberg, T. (2003). Substance abuse in the rural community. In B. Hudnall-Stamm (Ed.), *Rural behavioral health care*. Washington, DC: American Psychological Association.

Chess, W. A., & Norlin, J. M. (1988). *Human behavior and the social environment: A social systems model*. Boston: Allyn and Bacon.

Ciarlo, J. A., & Zelarney, P. T. (2000). Focusing on the frontier: Isolated rural America. *Journal of Washington Academy of Sciences, 28,* 673–676.

Committee on School Health (2004). School-based mental health services. *American Academy of Pediatrics, 113(6),* 1839–1845.

Conger, R. D. (1997). The special nature of rural America. In E. Robertson, Z. Sloboda, G. M. Boyd, L. Beatty, & N. J. Kozel (Eds.), *Rural substance abuse: State of knowledge and issues* (National Institute on Drug Abuse Research Monograph No. 168, National Institutes of Health Publication No 97-4177, pp. 6–36). Washington, DC: US Government Printing Office.

Cook, P. J., & Mizer, K. L. (1994). ERS typology revised and updated. *Rural Development Perspectives, 9(3),* 38–42.

Daley, M. R. (2015). *Rural social work in the 21st century.* Chicago: Lyceum Books.

Davenport, J. A., & Davenport, J. (1995). Rural social work. *Encyclopedia of social work* 19th ed; (pp. 2076–2085). Washington, DC: NASW Press.

Davenport, J. A., & Davenport, J. III. (2008). Rural practice. In T. Mizrahi, & L. E. Davis (Eds.), *Encyclopedia of social work* (20th ed.; pp. 536–541). Washington, DC: NASW Press & New York: Oxford University Press.

Dolgoff, R., Harrington, D., & Loewenberg, F. M. (2012). Brooks/Cole *Empowerment Series: Ethical decisions in social work practice.* Belmont, CA: Thomson Brooks/Cole.

Durham, J. A., & Miah, M. M. R. (1993). Social work in a rural health care setting: Farm families. *Human Services in the Rural Environment, 17(2),* 9–13.

Edwards, M. E., Torgerson, M., & Sattem, J. (2009). Paradoxes of providing rural social services: The case of homeless youth. *Rural Sociology, 74(3)*, 330–355.

Eichler, M. (2007). *Consensus organizing: Building communities of mutual self-interest.* Thousand Oaks, CA: Sage Publications.

Fitzsimons, N. M., Hagemeister, A. K., & Braun, E. J. (2011). Interpersonal violence against people with disabilities: Understanding the problem from a rural context. *Journal of Social Work in Disability & Rehabilitation, 10(3)*, 166–188, doi:10.1080/1536710X.2011.596437

Fortney, J., Rost, K., Zhang, M., & Warren, J. (1999). The impact of geographic accessibility on the intensity and quality of depression treatment. *Medical Care, 37(9)*, 884–893.

Friedman, T. L. (2005). *The world is flat: A brief history of the twenty-first century.* New York: Farrar, Straus, and Giroux.

Ginsberg, L. H. (Ed.) (1998). *Social work in rural communities* (3rd ed.). Washington, DC: CSWE Press.

Ginsberg, L. H. (2005). Introduction: The overall context of rural practice. In L. H. Ginsberg (Ed.), *Social work in rural communities* (4th ed.) (pp. 1–14). Alexandria, VA: Council on Social Work Education, Inc.

Ginsberg, L. H. (Ed.) (2011). *Social work in rural communities* (5th ed.). Washington, DC: CSWE Press.

Green, R. (2003). Social work in rural areas: A personal and professional challenge. *Australian Social Work, 56(3)*, 209–219.

Green, R. K., Johnson, A. K., Bremseth, M. D., & Tracy, E. (1995). No home, no family: Homeless children in Ohio. *Human Services in the Rural Environment, 19(2/3)*, 9–13.

Greene, R. R. (2000). *Human behavior theory and social work practice* (2nd ed.). New Brunswick, NJ: Aldine Transaction.

Greene, R. R., & Blundo, R. G. (1999). Postmodern critique of systems theory in social work with the aged and their families. *Journal of Gerontological Social Work, 31(3/4)*, 87–100.

Gumpert, J. (1985). A model for group work practice in rural areas. *Social Work with Groups, 8(3)*, 49–57.

Gumpert, J., & Saltman, J. E. (1998). Social group work practice in rural areas: The practitioners speak. *Social Work with Groups, 21(3)*, 19–34.

Hardcastle, D. A. (1985). Rural stereotypes and professional caregivers. *Arete, 10(2)*, 73–82.

Hardcastle, D. A., & Powers, P. R. (2004). *Community practice: Theories and skills for social workers.* Cambridge: Oxford University Press.

Hargrove, D. S. (1982). An overview of professional considerations in the rural community. In P. A. Keller & J. D. Murray (Eds.), *Handbook of rural community health.* New York: Human Services Press.

Hartman, A. (1995). Diagrammatic assessment of family relationships. *Families in Society, 76(2)*, 111–122.

Haxton, J. E., & Boelk, A. Z. (2010). Serving families on the frontline: Challenges and creative solutions in rural hospice social work. *Social Work in Health Care, 49*, 526–550. doi:10.1080/00981381003648422

Henderson, D.A., & Tickamyer, A. R. (2008). Lost in Appalachia: The unexpected impact of welfare reform on older women in rural communities. *Journal of Sociology & Social Welfare, 35(3)*, 153–171.

Hepworth, D. H., Rooney, R. H., Rooney G. D., Strom-Gottfried, K., & Larsen, J. (2006). *Direct social work practice: Theory and skills.* Belmont, CA: Thomson Brooks/Cole.

Hepworth, D. H., Rooney, R. H., Rooney G. D., Strom-Gottfried, K., & Larsen, J. (2013). *Direct social work practice: Theory and skills.* Belmont, CA: Thomson Brooks/Cole.

Hilton, T., & DeJong, C. (2010). Homeless in God's country: Coping strategies and felt experiences of the rural homeless. *Journal of Ethnographic and Qualitative Research, 5(1)*, 12–30.

Hsieh, H. H., Cheng, S-C., Sharma, A., Sanders, R. A., & Thiessen, C. (1989). The relation of rural alcoholism to farm economy. *Community Mental Health Journal, 25(4)*, 341–347.

Hudson, C. G. (2000). At the edge of chaos: A new paradigm for social work? *Journal of Social Work Education, 36(2)*, 1–17.

Humble, M. N., Lewis, M. L., Scott, D. L., & Herzog, J. R. (2013). Challenges in rural social work practice: When support groups contain your neighbors, church members, and the PTA, *Social Work with Groups, 36:2–3*, 249–258. doi: 10.1080/01609513.2012 .753807.

Jacob, S., Willits, F. K., & Jensen, L. (1996). Residualism and rural America: A decade later. *Journal of Sociology and Social Welfare, 23(3)*, 151–162.

Jensen, L. (2006). New immigrant settlements in rural America: Problems, prospects and policies. Durham, NH: Carsey Institute, University of New Hampshire. Retrieved from http://www.carseyinstitute.unh.edu/publications/Report_Immigration.pdf.

Jerrell, J. M. (1983). Work satisfaction among rural mental health staff. *Community Mental Health Journal, 19*, 187–200.

Johnson, L. C. (1998). *Social work practice: A generalist approach* (6th ed.). Boston: Allyn & Bacon.

Judd, F. K., Jackson, H. J., Komiti, A., Murray, G., Hodgins, G., & Fraser, C. (2002). High prevalence disorders in urban and rural communities. *Australian and New Zealand Journal of Psychiatry, 36*, 104–113.

Kaplan, D. W., Calonge, B. N., Guernsey, B. P., & Hanrahan, M. B. (1998). Managed care and school-based health centers: Use of health services. *Archives of Pediatric & Adolescent Medicine, 152(1)*, 25–33.

Karis, J., & Wandrei, K. (Eds.) (1996). *Person-in-Environment System: The P.I.E. Classification System for Social Functioning Problems* (3-21). Washington DC: NASW Press.

Kirst-Ashman, K. K., & Hull, G. H. Jr. (2001). *Generalist practice with organizations and communities*. Belmont, CA: Brooks/Cole.

Landis, P. H. (1936). The new deal and rural life. *American Sociological Review, 1(4)*, 592–603.

Lane, K., & Judd, L. (1990). Group intervention with children living in a rural area during the farm economic crisis. *Human Services in the Rural Environment 13(3)*, 33–36.

Larson, J. E. (June, 2009). Rural, grassroots community organizing brings a dental home to those in need. Northern Access Dental Center, Bemidji, MN. Retrieved from http://156.98.150.11/divs/orhpc/conf/2009/presentations/5c.pdf

Leighninger, R. D., Jr. (1977). Systems theory and social work: A reexamination. *Journal of Education for Social Work, 13(3)*, 44–49.

Lengerich, R. (2012, January 22). Nation's top three poorest counties in Western South Dakota. *Rapid City Journal*. Retrieved from http://rapidcityjournal.com

Lewis, M. L., Scott, D. L., & Calfee, C. (2013). Rural social service disparities and creative social work solutions for rural families across the life span. *Journal of Family Social Work, 16,* 101–115. doi: 10.1080/10522158.2012.747118

Lofquist, D., Lugaila, T., O'Connell, M., & Feliz, S. (2012). Households and Families: 2010. *2010 Census Briefs*. Washington, DC: U.S. Census Bureau.

Lohmann, N., & Lohmann, R. A. (Eds.) (2005). *Rural social work practice.* New York: Columbia University Press.

Longworth, R. C. (2008). *Caught in the middle: America's heartland in the age of globalism.* New York: Bloomsbury USA.

Lovelace, O. (1995). Stress in rural America. *Journal of Agromedicine, 2(2),* 71–78.

Mackie, P. F. E. (2007). Understanding educational and demographic differences between rural and urban social workers. *Journal of Baccalaureate Social Work, 12(3),* 114–128.

Mackie, P. F. E. (2008). Are social workers really burned out? An analysis between rural and urban social workers. *Journal of Rural Mental Health, 32(2),* 3–18.

Mackie, P. F. E. (2009). Grassroots community practice: Applying Alinsky's rules in the 21st century. *Reflections: Narratives of Professional Helping, 15(3),* 47–59.

Mackie, P. F. E. (2011). Rural social work recruitment and retention challenges: Why is it so difficult to fill rural social work positions? In L. Ginsberg (Ed.), *Social work in rural communities* (5th ed.). Alexandria, VA: CSWE Press.

Mackie, P. F. E. (2012). Social work in a very rural place: A study of practitioners in the Upper Peninsula of Michigan. *Journal of Contemporary Rural Social Work, 4,* 63–90. Online http://journal.und.edu/crsw/issue/view/28

Mackie, P. F. E. (2015). Technology in rural behavioral health care practice: Policy concerns and solution suggestions. *Journal of Rural Mental Health, 39,* 5–12. doi: 10.1037/rmh0000027

Mackie, P. F. E., & Leibowitz, G. (2013). Teaching community organizing? A postmodernist comparison between Alinsky's conflict and Eichler's consensus models. *Journal of Baccalaureate Social Work, 18,* 73–88.

Mackie, P. F. E., & Lips, R. A. (2010). Is there really a problem with hiring rural social service staff? An exploratory study among social service supervisors in rural Minnesota. *Families in Society, 91(4),* 433–439.

Mackie, P. F. E., & Simpson, C. L. (2007). Factors influencing undergraduate social work students' perceptions about rural-based practice: A pilot study. *Journal of Rural Mental Health, 31(2),* 5–21.

Mallon, B., & Houstra, T. (2007). Telephone technology in social work group treatment. *Social Work, 32(2),* 139–141.

Martinez-Brawley, E. E. (2000). *Close to home: Human services and the small community.* Washington, DC: NASW Press.

Martinez-Brawley, E. E., & Blundall, J. (1989). Farm families' preferences toward the personal social services. *Social Work, November,* 513–522.

Matthews, H. J. (1927). Special problems in social work. *Social Forces, 6(1),* 67–73.

Merikangas, K. R., He, J., Burstein, M., Swanson, S. A., Avenevoli, S., Cui, L., Benjet, C., Georgiades K., & Swendsen J. (2010). Lifetime prevalence of mental disorders in U.S. adolescents: Results from the National Comorbidity Study-Adolescent Supplement (NCS-A). *Journal of the American Academy of Child and Adolescent Psychiatry, 49(10),* 980–989.

Mermelstein, J., & Sundet, P. (1977). Community control and the determination of professional role in rural mental health. In *Human Services in the Rural Environment Reader.* Madison, WI: University of Wisconsin—Extension Service.

Meystedt, D. M. (1984). Religion and the rural population: Implications for social work. *Social Casework, 65(4),* 219–226.

Miller, K. K., & Weber, A. B. (2004). How does persistent poverty dynamics and demographics vary across the rural-urban continuum? *Measuring Rural Diversity, 1,* 1–7.

National Association of Social Workers (2013). Code of Ethics. Washington, DC. Retrieved from https://www.socialworkers.org/pubs/code/default.asp

National Health Service Corp (2015). Loans and scholarships. Retrieved from http://www.hrsa.gov/loanscholarships/index.html

Neighborworks America (2011). Rural development Symposium 2005. The new rural America: Partners in progress. San Francisco. Retrieved from http://nw.org/network/training/upcoming/ruralSymposium05.asp

Nemon, H. (2007). Community action: Lessons from forty years of federal funding, antipoverty strategies, and participation of the poor. *Journal of Poverty, 11*, 1–22. doi: 10.1300/J134v11n01

Nooe, R. M., & Cunningham, M. L. (1992). Rural dimensions of homelessness: A rural-urban comparison. *Human Services in the Rural Environment, 15(4)*, 5–9.

Orleck, A., & Hazirjian, L. G. (2011). *War on Poverty: A new grass-roots history, 1964–1980.* Athens, GA: University of Georgia Press.

Oser, C. B., Biebel, E. P., Pullen, E. L., & Harp, K. L. H. (2011). The influence of rural and urban substance abuse treatment counselor characteristics on clients' outcomes. *Journal of Social Service Research, 37*, 390–402. doi: 10.1080/01488376.2011.582020.

Panelli, R. (2006). Rural society. In P. Cloke, T. Marsden, & P. T. Mooney (Eds.), *Handbook of rural studies.* Thousand Oaks, CA: Sage Publications Ltd.

Pedeliski, T. B. (2011). Buffalo commons. Encyclopedia of the Great Plains [Online]. Retrieved from http://plainshumanities.unl.edu/encyclopedia/doc/egp.ii.008.

Pew Research Center's Forum on Religion & Public Life. (2010). U.S. religious landscape survey. Retrieved from http://www.pewforum.org/PewForum/Use-Policy.aspx

Popper, D. E., & Popper, F. J. (1987). Great Plains: From dust to dust. *Planning, 53*, 12–18.

Popple, P. R., & Leighninger, L. (2008). *The policy-based profession: An introduction to social welfare policy analysis for social workers.* Boston: Pearson/Allyn & Bacon.

Ray, R. A., & Street, A. F. (2005). Who's there and who cares: Age as an indicator of social support networks for caregivers among people living with motor neurone disease. *Health & Social Care in the Community, 13(6)*, 542–552. doi: 10.1111/j.1365-2524.2005.00586.x

Ricketts, T. C. (1999). *Rural health in the United States*. New York: Oxford University Press.

Riebschleger, J. (2007). Social workers' suggestions for effective rural practice. *Families in Society, 88(2)*, 203–213.

Rosmann, M. R. (2011). *Excellent joy: Fishing, farming, hunting, and psychology*. North Liberty, IA: Ice Cube Press.

Rost, K., Owen, R., Smith, J., & Smith, G. (1998). Rural-urban difference in service use and course of illness in bipolar disorder. *Journal of Rural Health, 14(1)*, 36–43.

Rounds, K. A. (1988). AIDS in rural areas: Challenges to providing care. *Social Work, 33*, 257–261.

Rounds, K. A., Galinsky, M. J., & Stevens, L. S. (1991). Linking people with AIDS in rural communities: The telephone group. *Social Work, 36(1)*, 13–18.

Rural Assistance Center (2015). What is rural? Retrieved from https://www.raconline.org/topics/what-is-rural

Rural Utilities Service (2011). Homepage. Retrieved from http://www.usda.gov/rus/

Saleeby, D. (1997). *The strengths perspective in social work*. New York: Longman Publishers.

Saltman, J., Gumpert, J., Allen-Kelly, K., & Zubrzycki, J. (2004). Rural social work practice in the United States and Australia, *International Social Work, 47(4)*, 515–531.

Sanderson, D. (1923). Community organization for rural social work. *Journal of Social Forces, 1(2)*, 156–161.

Scales, T. L., & Streeter, C. L. (2004). *Rural social work: Building and sustaining community assets*. Belmont, CA: Brooks/Cole/ Thomson Publishing.

Schank, J. A., & Skovholt, T. M. (2006). *Ethical practice in small communities: Challenges and rewards for psychologists*. Washington, DC: American Psychological Association.

Shandy, D. J., & Fennelly, K. (2006). A comparison of the integration experiences of two African immigrant populations in a rural community. *Journal of Religion & Spirituality in Social Work, 25(1)*, 23–45.

Shaw, M. E., & Costanzo, P. R. (1982). *Theories of social psychology*. Auckland: McGraw-Hill International.

Sheridan, K. (2014). A systematic review of the literature regarding family context and mental health of children from rural methamphetamine-involved families: Implications for rural child welfare practice. *Journal of Public Child Welfare, 8(5)*, 514–538. doi:10.1080/15548732.2014.948584

Siporin, M. (1980). Ecological systems theory in social work. *Journal of Sociology and Social Welfare, 7(7)*, 507–532.

Slovak, K., Sparks, A., & Hall, S. (2011). Attention to rural populations in social work's scholarly journals. *Journal of Social Service Research, 37(4)*, 428–438. doi: 10.1080/01488376.2011.578035

Stamm, B. H. (2003). *Rural behavioral health care.* Washington, DC: American Psychological Association Press.

Steiner, J. F. (1921). Education for social work. *The American Journal of Sociology, 26(6)*, 744–766.

Steiner, J. F. (1926). The basis of procedure in rural social work. *Social Forces, 4(3)*, 504–509.

Stone, G. (2011). Technology in rural social work practice. In L. Ginsberg (Ed.), *Social work in rural communities* (5th ed.; pp. 87–110). Washington, DC: Council on Social Work Education Press.

Summers, G. (1998). Minorities in rural society. In L. Ginsberg (Ed.), *Social work in rural communities* (3rd ed.). Washington, DC: CSWE Press.

Sun, F. (2011). Community service use by older adults: The roles of sociocultural factors in rural-urban differences. *Journal of Social Service Research, 37(2)*, 124–135. doi:10.1080/01488376. 2011.547446

Swanson, M. (1972). Professional social work in America. *Agricultural History, October, XLVI(4)*, 515–527.

Swerdlik, M., Rice, W., & Larson, E. (1978). The effect of a group therapy experience on fifth grade acting out boys. *School Social Work Journal, 2(2)*, 83–88.

Taras, H. L. (2004). American Academy of Pediatrics, Committee on School Health: School based mental health services. *Pediatrics, 113(6)*, 1839–1845.

Tonnies, F. (1963). *Community and society.* New York: Harper & Row.

Toseland, R. W. (2009). Telephone groups. In A. Gitterman & R. Salmon (Eds.), *Encyclopedia of social work with groups* (pp. 314–317). New York: Routledge.

Toseland, R. W., & Horton, H. (2008). Group work. In T. Mizrahi & L. E. Davis (Eds.), *Encyclopedia of social work* (20th ed). Washington, DC: NASW Press & New York: Oxford University Press.

Toseland, R. W., & Rivas, R. F. (2012). *An introduction to group work practice* (7th ed.). Boston, MA: Pearson Education, Inc.

Ulrich, J. (2010). How Yoopers see the future of their communities: Why residents leave or stay in Michigan's Upper Peninsula. Policy Brief No. 17, Carsey Institute. University of New Hampshire, pp. 1–9. Retrieved from http://www.carseyinstitute.unh.edu/publications/PB_Ulrich_Yoopers.pdf

United States Census Bureau (2015a). Urban and rural classification. Retrieved from http://www.census.gov/geo/reference/urban-rural.html

United States Census Bureau (2015b). State and county quick facts: Shannon County, South Dakota. Retrieved from http://quickfacts.census.gov/qfd/states/46/46113.html.

United States Department of Agriculture (USDA) Farm Bill. Farm Bill 2008. Retrieved from http://www.usda.gov/wps/portal/usda/farmbill2008?navid=FARMBILL2008

United States Department of Agriculture Office of Rural Development (USDA) (2011). *About RD.* Retrieved from http://www.rurdev.usda.gov/Home.html

United States Department of Agriculture Office of Rural Development (2013). Homepage. Washington, DC. Retrieved from http://www.rurdev.usda.gov/Home.html

Vidich, A. J., & Bensman, J. (1960). *Small town in mass society.* Garden City, NY: Doubleday & Doubleday, Inc. Anchor Books.

Vodde, R., & Giddings, M. (2000). The field system eco-map. *The Journal of Teaching in Social Work, 20(3–4),* 41–61, doi:10.1300/J067v20n03_05

Wagenfeld, M. O., Murray, J. D., Mohatt, D. F., & DeBruyn, J. C. (1994). Mental health and rural America: 1980–1993. An overview and annotated bibliography (NIH Publication No. 94-3500). Washington, DC: Office of Rural Health Policy (HRSA) and Office of Rural Mental Health Research (NIMH).

Waltman, G. H. (1986). Main street revisited: Social work practice in rural areas. *Social Casework, 67(8)*, 466–474.

Waltman, G. H. (2011). Reflections on rural social work. *The Journal of Contemporary Social Services, 92(2)*, 236–239. doi: 10.1606/1044-3894.4091

Watkins, T. R. (2004). Natural helping networks: Assets for rural communities. In T. L. Scales & C. L. Streeter (Eds.), *Rural social work: Building and sustaining community assets* (pp. 65–76). Belmont, CA: Brooks/Cole.

Weiss-Gal, I. (2008). The Person-In-Environment approach: Professional ideology and practice of social workers in Israel. *Social Work, 53(1)*, 65–75.

Wellstone, P. (1978). *How the rural poor got power: Narrative of a grass-roots organizer.* Amherst, MA: University of Massachusetts Press.

Winer, M. B., & Ray, K. (1994). *Collaboration handbook: Creating, sustaining, and enjoying the journey.* St. Paul, MN: Amherst H. Wilder Foundation.

York, R. O., Denton, R. T., & Moran, J. R. (1989). Rural and urban social work practice: Is there a difference? *Social Casework, 70*, 201–209.

Zapf, M. K. (2009). Rural regions. In A. Gitterman & R. Salmon (Eds.), *Encyclopedia of social work with groups* (pp. 272–275). New York: Routledge.

Zellmer, D. D., & Anderson-Meger, J. I. (2011). Rural Midwestern religious beliefs and help seeking behavior: Implications for social work practice. *Social Work & Christianity, 38(1)*, 29–50.

Index

About the Authors

Paul Force-Emery Mackie (MSW, *Washington University in St. Louis;* PhD, University of Denver) is professor of social work at Minnesota State University, Mankato. He currently serves as President of the National Association for Rural Mental Health (NARMH) (2015-2017) and has been on the NARMH Board of Directors since 2009. He has written extensively on rural behavioral health labor force challenges and issues.

Kimberly Zammitt (BSW, MSW, *University of Southern Mississippi;* PhD, *Jackson State University*) is professor of social work at Minnesota State University, Mankato. With over ten years of clinical social work practice experience in the fields of community mental health, child and adolescent mental health, and geriatric mental health, Zammitt has worked throughout the state of Mississippi establishing behavioral health services in skilled nursing and assisted living facilities. She served as clinical social worker and training specialist working to bring mental health services to individuals, families, and groups in remote rural areas in Mississippi. This position included supervision of field students and training of professional staff. Prior to that, Zammitt worked as a therapist coordinator at a child and adolescent day treatment program.

Michelle Alvarez (MSW, *University of Maryland at Baltimore;* EdD, *Nova Southeastern University*) is associate Dean of Social Sciences, College of Online and Continuing Education at Southern New Hampshire University. She taught in two rural MSW programs at Minnesota State University, Mankato and the University of Southern Indiana. She was the co-coordinator for field at MSU, Mankato and appreciated the support from many agencies who were spread out across the rural towns in Minnesota and surrounding states. This book is dedicated to those students and practitioners whose passion is to provide services in rural areas.